INNOCENT III

Vicar of Christ or Lord of the World?

PROBLEMS IN EUROPEAN CIVILIZATION

INNOCENT III

Vicar of Christ or Lord of the World?

EDITED WITH AN INTRODUCTION BY

James M. Powell

UNIVERSITY OF ILLINOIS

D. C. HEATH AND COMPANY · BOSTON

Englewood · Indianapolis · Dallas · Burlingame · Atlanta

Table of Contents

Introduction

INNOCENT III (1198–1216) ruled the Church during a crucial period in its history. Western Europe was spilling over into the Islamic world as a result of the Crusades. The feudal and manorial regimes were weakening their hold on political and economic life in the West as merchants and townsmen escaped their control by securing royal protection or by forming virtually independent communes. Monarchs in the West were seizing the effective reins of government and beginning to create more centralized territorial states. The traditional currents of mediaeval intellectual life were beginning to flow in new directions under the impetus of Aristotelian and Arab learning. Numerous heretical sects, some caused by and some reacting against these changes in the social order, preached anti-materialist doctrines to a Christendom growing more materialistic by the day. These new ideas disturbed the delicate equilibrium which the mediaeval Church had attempted to maintain between the City of God and the City of Man. In the tension between these two poles there was evidence of a potential split in the personality of mediaeval man. The Church worked to prevent this split. Committed by its founder to the mission of leading men to the heavenly city, it nevertheless showed a remarkable awareness of man's earthly needs. In the late twelfth and early thirteenth centuries, near-revolutionary pressures threatened the traditional bases of mediaeval society. The Church, universal and all-pervasive, needed leadership to meet the challenge and found it in Innocent III.

From his accession in 1198 until his death in June, 1216, Innocent worked unceasingly on all fronts to defend ecclesiastical rights and privileges, to combat heresy, to reform the Church in administration and morals, and to meet the challenge of a changing social order. The durability of his achievements during this crucial period is the best measure of his significance for the history of Europe and the whole of western civilization. The Church, which he defended so well, remained and remains today not only an important factor in the history of religion, but also a significant force in our society. It weathered the Protestant Reformation, the greatest challenge to its existence in its history. Moreover, Innocent's determination to protect the rights of the Church acted in retrospect as a deterrent to the rise of absolutism and to the triumph of absolutist theories of the state. If not the greatest of the mediaeval popes, Innocent at least ruled the Church at the height of its power. Did he, in his attempts to carry out his many-directioned policies, perhaps exceed the traditional limits of papal authority? Before we can hope to answer this question, it would be well to examine the nature of papal claims in the centuries prior to Innocent's accession to the papal throne.

The papacy had gained tremendous power in the course of the Middle Ages. Popes, from the fifth century onward, had gradually won recognition for their claim to leadership in the western Church and, for brief periods, even in the East. Leo I (440–461) had worked assiduously to extend papal jurisdiction over bishops. His major problem was to gain recognition of

Rome's claims to primacy from a higher clergy long accustomed to solely local co-operation. Even at this early period, however, relations between spiritual and temporal authorities needed defining. Since the age of Constantine, Roman emperors in the East had exerted a pre-eminent influence over the affairs of the Church. Gelasius I, Pope from 492 to 496, faced this question squarely in his letter to the Emperor Anastasius and, in doing so, laid down the position that came to be widely accepted by the popes of the early Middle Ages. He maintained that the power of priests was greater than that of temporal rulers because the clergy had to answer to God even for the souls of kings. The Gelasian theory thus gave the papacy wide scope for the development of claims to act in the temporal sphere. Moreover, the actual power of the popes to act in secular affairs received an added impetus from the power vacuum created in the West by the decline of Roman authority. In the West, especially in Italy, the pope stood as the symbol of a universal society transcending divisions among barbarian tribes.

The seventh and eighth centuries saw even this symbol of unity besieged. Only the energetic action of the Catholic Frankish monarchy saved the papacy from the chaos of Italian and Roman politics. But the price exacted by the Franks was almost too great. Their influence, especially under Charlemagne, became so paramount in ecclesiastical affairs that the pope was reduced almost to the status of court chaplain. It is not surprising, therefore, that the withdrawal of this strong protection as a result of the decline of the Carolingians found the papacy unable to exert leadership in a society increasingly more decentralized and feudal. Corruption spread through the whole organism of the Church as bishoprics and abbacies came under control of lay feudal lords. Spiritual-minded churchmen responded to these conditions by espousing the cause of reform. Gradually, the demand for reform grew more articulate and drew significant support, particularly from the monks of Cluny, a monastery in eastern France, founded in the tenth century and owing allegiance to no feudal lord. The Cluniacs early recognized the need for centralized leadership in the Church and dedicated themselves to strengthening the power of a reformed papacy. From Leo IX (1049–1054) to Gregory VII (1073–1085) a succession of reformers occupied the papal throne and asserted the right of Rome to control the election of bishops and to dismiss those who had failed in the duties of their office. They promoted celibacy among the clergy with some success and vigorously condemned simony, the practice of buying and selling ecclesiastical offices, an abuse which had become rampant with feudal control of churches and monasteries. The reform popes directed considerable effort to improving the administrative machinery of the Church so that their decrees could be carried out more effectively. This period also saw the beginnings and early growth of canon law, which formulated many of the aims of the reformers. The climax of this movement came with the Investiture Controversy, in which Gregory VII and his successors fought to prevent the Emperor Henry IV from keeping control of the appointment of bishops and abbots. The issue was greater, however, than a question of ecclesiastical rights; on its solution depended the future of both Church and Empire, for the bishops had come to play an important role in both secular and ecclesiastical administration in Germany. Though there was no clear-cut victory for the Church, the Concordat of Worms in 1122 was a profound blow to the prestige of the Empire. Not even the efforts of Frederick Barbarossa were sufficient to overcome the will of the papacy to establish its undisputed hegemony over Christendom. The reform movement had forged the strength of the papacy and paved the way for Innocent III. Trained as a canon lawyer and theologian, from very early in his life at the center of church affairs,

Innocent III was uniquely suited to carry on the tradition of a strong papacy.

From the very first days of his reign Innocent spoke out on the subject of papal power. Though he referred to himself as a servant, he claimed for his office the fullness of power. Moreover, he pursued an extremely active policy which made it plain that he did not claim what he was not willing to seek. The pursuit of his goal to make papal power effective brought him into conflict with emperors and kings, against whom he did not hesitate to threaten and to use ecclesiastical censures in order to secure obedience. Moreover, in the Franciscan Order, Innocent left an enduring monument to his ability to make use of popular movements and, in the Dominican Order, to his zeal for purity of doctrine. Under him, Rome became the focal point not only of ecclesiastical administration, but also of many problems whose ecclesiastical connection was tenuous. Under his leadership, too, papal administration reached the height of its effectiveness. Certainly Innocent's success was in large measure the result of policies formulated by his predecessors, but this fact must not cause us to overlook the role of this great pope. He bequeathed to his successors a papal machinery more vast and complex than any that had ever existed, and with it a legacy of claims and accomplishments to serve as precedents for future action. Within a century of his death, Boniface VIII was stating the right of the papacy and the clergy to be completely free of secular control. That claim was put to the test in the France of Philip the Fair and failed. But much of Innocent's work did not fail; the Church weathered all storms, even the Reformation. Only one question remains. Did Innocent exceed the traditional limits of papal authority to achieve his goals? Can all theories of temporal authority put forward by his successors and their partisans be traced to him?

The contemporaries of Innocent III were not unanimous in either condemning or supporting him. Walther von der Vogelweide, the German poet of the early thirteenth century and a great partisan of the Empire, was only one of many who adopted an anticlerical and anti-Italian tone in their writings. This attitude persisted in the writings of fourteenth- and fifteenth-century authors and became current bill-of-fare among some humanists and the Protestant reformers. Wherever anticlericalism or Protestantism flourished, their proponents united in laying at Innocent's door the blame for founding the papal monster they so abhorred. In this way the most commonly held view of Innocent's ideas on the relationship between the spiritual and temporal authority was formed.

The majority of historians writing in the nineteenth century adopted the view that Innocent III had aimed at establishing a papal world-state so that the pope could dominate all temporal concerns of men. Conservative Catholic historians, well represented by Friedrich Hurter, did not deny papal activity in the temporal sphere. Hurter argued, however, that the Pope had worked for the common good, a higher goal than that of ambitious and sinful kings. As protector of the common good, Innocent therefore had the duty to interfere in secular matters. He was, in fact, over kings. But Hurter's arguments made no significant inroads into the majority position. When Albert Hauck published his history of the Church in Germany at the turn of the century, he made no concessions to Hurter's view of Innocent. Concerning the accession of Innocent III to the papal throne, Hauck was able to assert: "Now is the Pope no more primarily priest, but before all a secular lord." [1] By this statement he meant that the pope was trying to transform "the moral and religious authority of the papacy into political power." [2] The basic difference between the Hurter view of Innocent's concept of temporal power and that

[1] Albert Hauck, *Kirchengeschichte Deutschlands,* IV (Leipzig, 1903), 685.
[2] *Ibid.,* IV, 744.

put forth by Hauck is not a denial of the papal claim to exercise authority in the temporal sphere, but a disagreement over the purpose for which the pope used that authority.

Modern scholarship on the life and reign of Innocent III begins with the appearance of Achille Luchaire's biography, *Innocent III,* published in Paris during the first decade of the twentieth century. Luchaire did not condone his subject's attempts to intervene in secular affairs, but he placed considerable emphasis on the pope's accomplishments in reforming the Church and formulating doctrine. Moreover, on the important question of Innocent's motivation for acting in seemingly non-spiritual matters, Luchaire's study revealed the complexity of the problems faced by the pope. It also showed that Innocent was not the intransigent theorist of papal power that had so long been assumed. Luchaire maintained that the pope tailored his policies to fit political realities rather than doctrinaire positions.

R. W. and A. J. Carlyle did not entirely reject Luchaire's image of Innocent the political realist, but they insisted in their monumental *Mediaeval Political Theory in the West* that he had "relied in his dealings with secular powers mainly on his authority as vicar of Christ." [3] Although they avoided an indictment of Innocent himself, they maintained that "it is in the Decretal letters of Innocent III that we must look for the ultimate sources of the extreme view of papal authority in temporal affairs which was developed in the second half of the thirteenth century." [4] The Carlyles attempted to show how Innocent had exploited all the various powers of the papal office. He had acted as protector of minors, punisher of heresy, judge of disobedience, peacemaker, guarantor of treaties, and feudal overlord. In each of these cases he was able to point to papal precedents which had established

[3] A. J. and R. W. Carlyle, *Mediaeval Political Theory in the West,* V (Edinburgh, 1928), 233.
[4] *Ibid.,* V, 318.

his authority to act, but it was the cumulative effect of his activity in each of these areas that put such great power in his hands. Thus, in the view of the Carlyles, the chief motivation impelling Innocent to act vigorously even in disputed cases was his conception of the papal office. He saw in that office the vicegerency of Christ reaching out to touch all aspects of human life.

The tendency to move away from a purely political explanation for Innocent's policies represented a major break with what might be called the "classic" view of those policies found in Hauck. Charles McIlwain, in his masterful *Growth of Political Thought in the West,* went farther than almost any previous author in rejecting any political motivation of the pope's activities. It is clear, he argued, that Innocent claimed an almost illimitable jurisdiction; but this jurisdiction was primarily spiritual and based on the pope's duty as vicar of God. McIlwain laid special emphasis on the notion that Innocent acted in temporal affairs only when a matter of sin was involved (*ratione peccati*). Thus, in McIlwain's opinion, the limit of papal jurisdiction was essentially moral rather than political, and the whole question of temporal authority was therefore bound up with the right of the papacy to act as a moral legislator for Christendom.

The appearance in 1940 of Michele Maccarrone's study of the sources and meaning of Innocent's ideas on Church and State added a new dimension to the discussion of the spiritual and temporal sovereignty of the papacy. Maccarrone attempted to cast doubt upon the usual interpretation of key passages, such as *fullness of power* and *vicar of Christ;* more than this, he tried to prove that these passages were susceptible of an interpretation referring solely to the spiritual authority of the papacy and had actually been understood and used by Innocent and his predecessors in this sense. With Maccarrone, these phrases took on a new significance, spiritual in nature and referring only to the spiritual mission with which Christ had charged Peter. There is no question of temporal sovereignty because there is no claim of it. Maccarrone carried the tendency to reject a political explanation for the papal claims to the point of a denial of the existence of the claims.

Few if any historians have followed Maccarrone the whole distance in accepting his contentions. When Augustin Fliche published the tenth volume of his *Histoire de l'Église* in 1950, he acknowledged Maccarrone's viewpoint, but made it clear in his conclusion that he did not accept it. He could see no reason to doubt that Innocent III had wished to control the actions of temporal rulers and even to create a political unity in Christendom under the hegemony of the papacy. He asserted, however, that Innocent's vision of this unity was spiritual, its purpose "to ensure, in religious unity, the defense and spreading of the Catholic faith and Christian morality." [5] Fliche, among all modern authors, stands closest to the position set forth by Friedrich Hurter in his acceptance of the temporal power as a reality and his belief that it was aimed at promoting the good of Christianity. But Fliche is also close to the view of the Carlyles and McIlwain in emphasizing the spiritual basis of Innocent's claims. Thus, in his view, the pope acted not only in the interest of the Church, but on an authority vested in the Church and especially in the office of the papacy. Innocent acted in the temporal order only in the sense that he concerned himself with mundane affairs and not in the sense that he exceeded the limits of spiritual authority.

Recent writers have felt the need to provide a better balanced picture of Innocent, to depict somewhat more than his political ruptures with emperors and kings and to spend more time on his character and spirituality as well as his efforts to reform

the Church. Helene Tillmann's biography attempts such a portrayal. Innocent emerges as one who did not always act from the most sublime motives, who even sought political ends, but also as one who was willing to sacrifice the political goal for the spiritual good.

Although the trend toward de-emphasis of Innocent's temporal aspirations has dominated the historiography of the twentieth century, it has not gained complete acceptance. The popular view of this great pope, mirrored in textbooks of mediaeval history as well as general European history, has been reluctant to accept the idea of spiritual motivation as a satisfactory explanation for Innocent's pursuit of temporal goals. Moreover, some scholars have voiced misgivings, even to the point of reasserting the concept of temporal motives in strong terms. Johannes Haller, in his history of the popes, viewed Innocent as Lord of the World and prince of the whole earth, interpreting these appellations in strongly political terms. Perhaps, as Brian Tierney suggested very recently, the last word on Innocent and the papal claims to temporal jurisdiction is yet to be spoken. Tierney himself certainly expressed dissatisfaction with the current trend of historiography on this subject and, in fact, rejected it for the most part. In his view, Innocent did accept the role of secular rulers as divinely ordered and also assumed the need for two hierarchies of administration, but believed that both culminated in the pope.

In the selections that follow there are some points that are contradictory, but many which are capable of resolution. As the student reads he will become aware of the differences in viewpoint among the various authors. In part these differences can be explained by varying religious, social, or political backgrounds. But variant environments do not explain everything. There is no single interpretation that can be fully labelled as "Catholic" or as "Protestant." Therefore, the student ought not to use this information as a basis for re-

[5] Augustin Fliche, *Histoire de l'Église depuis les Origines à nos Jours*, X (Paris, 1950), 213.

jecting one view or another; rather he should look for the positive contribution made by each author. In this way, he will arrive at an understanding of the complex problem that each of these authors has attempted to interpret: What was Innocent III's conception of the limits of papal power?

The following selections are reprinted without the footnotes which appeared in the originals. Bibliographical data for references in the selections to various authors and their works will be found in the Suggestions for Additional Reading *at the end of this book. The student should familiarize himself with the terms in the Glossary before reading.*

GLOSSARY

ALBIGENSIAN   See CATHARI

ANATHEMA   A solemn ban issued by the church and accompanied by excommunication.

BULL   A papal letter sealed with a leaden seal, or *bulla*. These letters are usually of greater importance than the general run of correspondence.

CANON   Literally, a rule. See CANON LAW. Canon may also refer to a group of clergy, often those attached to a Cathedral, who follow a rule of life. This group acts as the electoral body for the selection of the bishop. Canons may also be used as a shortened form for canon laws.

CANON LAW   The law of the church.

CATHARI   A group of Provençal heretics who espoused a form of dualistic religion. Although Christ figured in their teachings, it is doubtful whether they could actually be called Christians. The heresy had its origins in the East and came to southern France from Bulgaria. Its relationship to the Manichaean heresy is not clear. See MANICHAEAN.

CELIBACY   The unmarried state. Celibacy of the clergy was advocated very early in the history of the church, especially in the West, but gained full acceptance only gradually.

CHAPTER   A meeting of monks or canons or other clergy. The term usually refers to the meeting at which a new abbot or bishop was elected.

CONCLAVE   The meeting at which the cardinals choose a new pope.

COUNCIL   A meeting of the bishops and prelates of the church to decide questions of faith and morals. A general or ecumenical council was usually summoned by the pope and presided over by his representatives. The Lateran Council, summoned by Innocent III in 1215, was a general council. See SYNOD.

CURIA   The Roman, or papal, curia is composed of the heads — usually cardinals — of the various administrative offices of the church.

DECRETAL   A decretal is a papal letter answering a question of Canon Law. Decretals is the name given to the collections of these letters.

ENCYCLICAL   A papal letter addressed to many bishops, princes, and lay people.

EXCOMMUNICATION   An ecclesiastical censure "cutting off" the person punished from communion with the faithful. There are various kinds or degrees of excommunication.

GLOSS   A marginal note or explanation. Glosses were the usual way in which commentators on canon law offered explanations of difficult points. Hence, the name Glossator, referring to a commentator on canon law.

HOMILETIC   Pertaining to a homily, or sermon.

INTERDICT   An ecclesiastical censure which forbids the holding of any church services in a particular area. A form of compulsion used by the church to enlist popular opinion against the persons censured.

MANICHAEAN   A heresy compounded of Persian dualism (Zoroastrianism) and Christianity which flourished in the fourth century A.D. St. Augustine of Hippo espoused the heresy during his youth, but later opposed it vigorously. The Manichaeans were especially strong in North Africa and the East.

PATRIMONY   This term usually refers in the text to the Patrimony of St. Peter, *i.e.*, the papal states.

PRIMACY   The claim of the pope to be supreme bishop, based in part on New Testament references and in part on the historical development of the church.

SIMONY   The buying and selling of ecclesiastical office.

SUFFRAGAN   A bishop who is subordinate to an Archiepiscopal See.

SYNOD   A local council, composed of the bishops from a certain area.

USURY   In mediaeval usage, all forms of interest on loans for consumption were usurious. Both church and state tried to enforce strong penalties for violations.

The Conflict of Opinion

. . . "for many centuries before and after Innocent, no one more learned, more pure in his way of life, more rich in merit to the Church and illustrious for great works sat on the throne of Saint Peter."

— FRIEDRICH HURTER

"Now is the Pope [Innocent] no more primarily priest, but before all a secular lord."

— ALBERT HAUCK

. . . "it seems clear that the jurisdiction claimed by Innocent III was almost illimitable and his exercise of it without parallel either in extent or effectiveness. Yet it was a jurisdiction in its nature primarily spiritual, and temporal only incidentally (*casualiter*), a power grounded on the Pope's duty as Vicar of God to judge of the sins (*de peccato*) of all Christians, not on his right as a temporal ruler to administer law for his subjects."

— CHARLES H. McILWAIN

"That [Innocent] wished to submit rulers to the control of the Holy See without otherwise mixing in their administration proper . . . , there is no doubt; but, if he desired the political unity of Christendom under the hegemony of the papacy, it was before all to ensure, in religious unity, the defense and the glory of the Catholic faith and Christian morality."

— AUGUSTIN FLICHE

"Innocent did take it for granted that, under the pope, secular rulers had a permanent and necessary role to play in the governance of Christian society, and that this role was a part of the divinely-ordered scheme of things. He assumed that two hierarchies were necessary for the government of the Christian world but, in his view, both hierarchies culminated in the pope."

— BRIAN TIERNEY

TWO VIEWS

Religion has played an important part in shaping the attitudes of historians toward Innocent III. In the first selection, Friedrich Hurter (1787–1865) indicts the Protestant-Rationalist interpretation for prejudice. Hurter, a staunch conservative, began the publication of his history of Innocent III in 1834, ten years before his conversion to Catholicism. In 1852, he became court historian at Vienna, a position he retained until his death.

Albert Hauck (1845–1918) studied at the Universities of Erlangen and Berlin. His academic career took him to Leipzig, where he edited the third edition of the *Realenzyklopädie für protestantische Theologie und Kirche* and taught theology. His outlook was Protestant and nationalist, a not uncommon combination among nineteenth- and early twentieth-century scholars in northern Germany.

Innocent III: Victim of Partisan Historians

FRIEDRICH HURTER

THE judgments of historians and writers, ancient and modern, who knew how to evaluate [Innocent] honestly on the basis of his accomplishments, the problems he solved, and his position as the central animator of his age, agree entirely in saying that for many centuries before and after [him] no one more learned, more pure in his way of life, more rich in merit to the Church, and illustrious for great works sat on the throne of Peter. No one after him possessed these qualities to such an extent, so that, save for Gregory VII, he was not only the most powerful, but also the wisest of popes — on a par with St. Bernard and Peter the Venerable, who knew how to surpass their age. He was praised by writers who witnessed his work and his influence on social life, because he spread Christianity in the North, restrained heresy in the South, subjected Constantinople to the Holy See (though the means may have been contrary to his intention), overcame the arrogance of the Moslems, and surpassed all in learning and devotion. In his writings he expressed joy at having lived in an age during which Christ granted victory to Christendom — while under the guidance of His faithful servant — over three enemies: schismatics, heretics, and infidels. Likewise, when he recalled the vain attempts of his predecessors, he was forced to render humble thanks to the Lord. He had, he said, by His command, cast nets for the fish and, with the aid of the friars in Livonia, won the pagans, converted the schismatics of Wallachia and Bulgaria, reunited Armenia — too long separated — and, finally, re-attached Greece to the Church. This is not to pretend that some were not made happy rather than sad by his death, because of the way he had pushed his influence, the intensity of his involvement in his work,

From Friedrich Hurter, *Storia di Papa Innocenzo III*, IV (Milan: Battezzati, 1858), IV, 346–9. Translated by the editor.

1

and the severity with which he governed. Recent authors take up the invectives of a few contemporaries and attach great importance to them without having a complete knowledge of his work and with less understanding of the feelings he revealed so many times in so many ways. But there is nothing strange about this fact; it is the result of the preconceived opinions and the sinister designs of these writers.

Other scholars have judged Innocent differently; if their representation of his position was valid, they knew how to rise above the prejudices of the age. The alterations or, at least, exaggerations, fruit of partisan spite, have not come from that group and ought not to be taken as historical truth. If, indeed, Innocent is accused of ambition for power, the solution depends on whether the authority he exercised, the way he mixed in secular affairs, the confidence with which he made the highest decisions in all cases, whether all this was for himself, for his own benefit, or for that single goal: his concept of duty and the importance of the papal office.

Innocent III Desired to Rule the World

ALBERT HAUCK

Not knowledge, but the feeling for order and rule, the prospects for reconciling incompatibles, and the cleverness to overcome all things in pursuit of a goal, make the ruler. To a high degree, Innocent possessed these gifts. The young cardinal was so little blinded by the splendor of the curia that he did not delude himself about the numerous abuses in its rule. Hardly was he pope than he ruthlessly reduced its size. Also, in these first days, he dismissed the swarm of servants that had collected under Celestine. To expedite the progress of business, he urged officials to work harder; he forbade them to demand presents for their services. The workshops in which false bulls were produced were forced to discontinue their profitable services. He paid special attention to the reorganization of the treasury. Nor did he overlook little things: under him, for the first time, the chancery collected fees for drawing up bulls; but he also knew how to manage important matters: one did not hear that the curia was overburdened by debts during his rule. As he ruled in Rome,

so in the Church and the world: subjectively and objectively, locally and universally, nothing escaped his notice. He knew how to win influence in all things. But in this thousandfold splintered occupation he never lost sight of the goal: the enforcement of papal rule in the Church and in the world.

He had not established the goal, but found it when he entered office. The ideology of the curia had known a long development. He had taken it over and restated it in the old formulas; even the proofs he used, the comparisons with which he illustrated it, were borrowed. But the borrowings sounded different, as the emphasis was put on this or that point. Here is a case in point. With Nicholas I, the statement of the supreme hegemony of the papacy arose out of the necessity to safeguard moral and religious interests; with Gregory VII, conviction of duty to accomplish Church reform provided the starting point. With Innocent, these points of reference were put aside; his goal was papal world dominion. Now was the pope no

From Albert Hauck, *Kirchengeschichte Deutschlands*, IV (Leipzig: Hinrichs'sche Buchhandlung), 684–691. Translated by the editor.

more primarily priest, but before all a secular lord. The language is concerned with his rule over Church and world, so before "Church" a "not only" should be introduced: not only the Church but also the world has been given to him to rule; so the latter appears in opposition to the former as the greater concern. Therefore, to Innocent, the essence of papal power was in the union of the priestly and the imperial dignity. In conformity with its origins and purpose, the imperial power belonged to the pope. Italy stood at the pinnacle of the world because Rome, as a result of its primacy, was the seat of priesthood and of kingship. It was logical for Innocent to take up the theory of the translation of the emperorship from the Greeks to the Romans by the popes. Now it won a more sure acceptance for the first time. It is still more remarkable that he stated the relationship of the two powers from the viewpoint of feudal law: the pope invested the candidate with the imperial power. It followed therefore that the pope had the right to examine the imperial election and to decide whether or not the candidate was fit for imperial office; and, again, the assertion that the pope should be empowered to raise an illegal candidate to the throne if he recognized him as the more suitable person was only one result. He treated princes in general as he did the emperors. That he allowed both to remain was a concession to actuality, not to any conviction that the secular power was necessary. His ideal was much more the immediate hegemony of the papacy in the world. Only if the secular and spiritual power were united in the hand of the pope could a situation completely satisfactory to the Church be established. Especially was this the natural situation for Italy.

We cannot deny that the assertion of an all-powerful papacy was at this point revolutionary. What was natural was exalted over historical right. Innocent had the courage to draw the conclusions of his viewpoint. Especially did his theory of the binding-force of oaths prove this point. It was

not enough that he conferred on the pope the right to repeal every oath according to his free judgment; he asserted that oaths sworn by princes generally were opposed to God and his precepts, *i.e.*, the papal commands, and were not binding. For it would not be permitted to him to hold the truth who would not hold God as the Truth. Therewith the permanence of all constitutional provisions of the secular power was left to the will and judgment of one man. The highest bishop of the Church was the absolute ruler in secular affairs. But, at the same time, the transformation of the papacy to a primarily secular power was accomplished.

Innocent was deeply conscious of the fact that he held this position. He identified himself consciously with hierarchical ideas. I, so he preached to the Roman people on the day of his consecration, I have been put over the house of God so that my honor like my office towers over all. Of me it has been said by the prophets: I will put you over peoples and kingdoms; I will give you the keys of the kingdom of heaven. The servant, who has been put in charge of the whole house, is the representative of Christ, the successor of Peter, the anointed of the Lord, the God of the Pharaohs; he is the mediator placed between God and men, lesser than God but greater than man. Innocent thought he was on such a lonely pinnacle that what was said of Christ in the Bible seemed to him to refer to himself as pope: his utterances were God's, his business was God's business. Already, a doubt about his intentions was a sin. Sinners did not have to answer secular judges on judgment day, but him, the pope.

One thinks of Innocent himself as a man who, from the ideas in his writings, lived in contempt of the world. Therefore, one must look for a tragic conflict between his intentions and his practices. But nowhere do we find a trace of it. For Innocent was no kindred soul of the poor man of Assisi; he was a man of this world, a man of great gifts, of sharp intelligence and unbending will, but also of strong individuality. Also, his friends have not denied that he could not endure opposition: he was violent and quick to anger. He thought himself above the pleasures of the world, so much did he deceive himself; unwillingly he confessed that he was fortunate because the papacy gave him the highest earthly rank; glory among men meant scarcely less to him than service before God. He thought and asserted that he had the unchangeable will to permit him to pursue the road of right; thus he also deceived himself in this. For, in general, he conducted business under the influence of preference and dislike. He liked France even as he hated Germany. In the former land the memories of a happy youth captivated him; in the latter he saw nothing but crudity and power. Likewise, devotion to his family blinded his moral judgment: he had no misgivings about enriching relatives from the wealth of the Church and he was prepared to sacrifice the claims of the Church in order to obtain the daughter of an emperor as wife for a nephew. He shielded his cousins in Rome by his authority, when they assassinated an enemy; there was no judge to bring them to account. Can one wonder that his political morality was all too open to criticism? He knew only one rule for politics, that of opportunity and what was opportune; he formed his opinions like a man who saw through men and esteemed them little. He was not afraid to appeal to their base impulses to get them to serve him. He knew that un-worthy men held church offices, but he put up with them, for their depravity would enslave them. Hypocrisy and deception were not offensive if they were in his service. On the other hand, he did not recognize the need for truthfulness in his political negotiations. As he undermined the purposes of enemies who could not protect themselves, so he gave assurances he knew he could not give; he managed events just as he needed them and, finally, was not afraid of open alliances. With moral scepticism, he believed that men of his kind tended to be the same: that he who seizes pitch besmirches himself seemed to him excuse enough.

Certainly Innocent was one of the most powerful of the Roman bishops. But he was not the ideal bishop that he has been judged by some; he belonged, however, in the procession of political popes. As the ecclesiastical idea of the papacy was, as it were, defeated in him by the idea of political hegemony, so also was his personality: he tended to speak in traditional religious formulae, but for his negotiations the rules of religion and morality were never unconditional law. We are informed that almost none of his contemporaries trusted him; his own Italians cast up to him his false deeds and his deceitfulness. They did not believe in his Italian patriotism, trotted out for show so ostentatiously. In Germany, they were convinced that he entertained the idea of destroying the empire. His death did nothing to alter this judgment.

A Realist Ascends the Papal Throne

ACHILLE LUCHAIRE

The name of Achille Luchaire (1846–1908) is one of the greatest among French historians. He taught at the University of Bordeaux and then at Paris, where he eventually succeeded Fustel de Coulange in the chair of Mediaeval History. In the present selection, Luchaire uses all his skill as an historian to re-create the events of Innocent III's accession to the papacy, while, at the same time, he carefully delineates the character, personality, and ambitions of the new pope.

A round and youthful visage with large eyes and high-arched eyebrows, a straight nose, and a small mouth. On the head, a cloth tiara, a simple pointed head-dress which ends in a tassel at the top and in a circle of metal at the bottom. On the breast, the insignia of the high priest, the pallium, a band of white wool sewn with red crosses. It is thus that the fragment of mosaic preserved in the villa of Duke Torlonia at Polì, and the painting from the underground church at Sacro Speco represent Innocent III. History adds that he was of small stature, agreeable appearance, had a facile tongue and a voice so sonorous and well-modulated that everyone listened and understood him even when he spoke in a low voice.

When we take the old Roman Road from Rome to Naples, we enter the valley of the River Sacco about ten miles from Rome. Above, on the foremost summits that surround the valley, the old Hernician towns, Segni, Anagni, Firentino, Palestrina, appear perched on the eternal seat of their cyclopean walls. Their churches have been built on the foundations of pagan temples. San Pietro of Segni, Santa Maria of Anagni, massive as fortresses, dominate still the stone houses and ramparts of their cities.

Here was the patrimony of Innocent III. The owners of the castle of Segni, of Lombard origin, had held the "county" of Roman Campagna since the tenth century. But it was only after Innocent III that, possessed of important properties in Rome and its environs, they came to use the surname "count," in Italian *conti*. This was the origin of the powerful Roman house of Conti, rival of the Orsini, the Colonna, and the Savelli. It is not surprising that it should have furnished several popes to the Christian world in the thirteenth century.

Lothario, or Lothar, of Segni was born in 1160 or 1161 at Anagni or Gavignano. Latin through his father, Trasmondo of Segni, and Roman through his mother, a member of the Scotti family, the future Innocent III was of a race of nobles and men of steel. Indeed, something of this remained in him: the greed of ambition, the warlike energy, the anger, the toughness. But an ecclesiastical education tempered, in this feudal man, the hereditary combativeness. Vowed to the clergy, he demonstrated a rare aptitude for learning. "He studied at Rome, Paris, and Bologna," according to his biographer or, rather, his panegyrist, the author of the *Gesta Innocentii Tertii* [The Deeds of Innocent III], "and he surpassed all his contemporaries by his success in philosophy, theology, and law."

We know little about his youth. At

From Achille Luchaire, *Innocent III* (Paris: Librairie Hachette, 1905), 1–34. Translated by the editor.

Rome his first master was Peter Ismaël, whom he named, in recognition of this fact, bishop of Sutri. He had better memory for the years he passed in the great international school of Paris. He took constant pleasure in France and Frenchmen. "It is to the University that I owe, by the grace of God, all the knowledge I have," he wrote to Philip Augustus. He asked Richard the Lion-Hearted for an archdeaconry for his former professor at Paris, the theologian Peter of Corbeil: "Master Peter, man of letters and savant of world renown, would be nothing to me were it not for his merits and his virtues. But how can I forget that I have followed his lessons and that he has taught me theology? I am not ashamed to say that I even pride myself in this." In 1198, he procured for him the bishopric of Cambrai. In 1200, he conferred on him the archbishopric of Sens in spite of the king of France and the Canons, partisans of another candidate. Peter of Corbeil was treated as an intruder by his clergy. But Innocent was obstinate: he preserved for his former teachers an affection that surpassed everything.

He did not, however, go so far as to tolerate their opposition. In 1203, while Peter of Corbeil was delaying the execution of the rigorous measures that the court of Rome had taken against a relative of Philip Augustus, Peter of Courtenai, Count of Auxerre, he received a thundering letter from the Lateran: "When we named you archbishop we thought we were doing something useful to the church of Sens and all France. In placing on the candlestick the light which was under a bushel, we thought we had given the service of God a pastor, not a mercenary. But behold, your lamp is out; it is no more than a smoking wick. You have hardly seen the wolf than you have let go your flock and fled; you have become like a mute dog that cannot bark." The archbishop took this remark so much to heart that Innocent felt obliged to console him: "It is only because everyone knows that I love you more than the other bishops of France

that I have chosen you to give an example to the whole episcopate." Master Peter had the desire: but the pope was far, the king was near, and when Philip Augustus became the uncontested master of the country after Bouvines [1214], it was expedient to be a royalist before all else. In 1216, with all his colleagues, the archbishop of Sens refused to accept the excommunication launched by Innocent against the king of France, who was blamed for encouraging his son to invade England. The Roman authority ordered an investigation into the disobedience of Peter of Corbeil. Unfortunate vicissitudes of policy! Death alone, perhaps, prevented the former scholar of Paris from excommunicating also his professor.

Nonetheless, Innocent remained the protector of the nascent University and its real head. It owed to him more than to the king the first privileges that gave it its independence. Interested in the good organization of the school where he had studied, he imposed on it regulations of intellectual and moral discipline. He defended it against abuses of power by the bishop and the chancellor of Notre Dame: "From my time," he wrote in 1212, "I have never seen that the scholars were treated in this fashion." And the suspension of 1213, ordered by the delegates whom he charged to bring peace between the University and the bishop, was a victory for the masters and the students. Beyond doubt, his policy acted to remove the great associations of scholars from the bishops and to make them instruments of the Roman power. But in his relations with the school of Paris, he was inspired by memories of his youth and by feelings of gratitude that he always proclaimed loudly. A great admirer of this University which he wished to be free and to flourish, he had the idea, after the founding of the Latin Empire of Constantinople [1204], of sending Paris professors to the Bosphorus to reform education there.

Bologna taught the young Lothar of Segni civil and canon law, the two sciences in which he excelled. After he became pope, he never forgot the canonists who were his masters or his companions in study. Huguccio of Pisa, bishop of Ferrara, one of his habitual correspondents, Peter Collivacino, his notary, Bernard of Pavia, and Sicard of Cremona received benefices, bishoprics, cardinalates, and missions of trust. The court of Innocent III was filled with lawyers and Bolognese men of law. A doctor of canon law, Gregory, was the principal executor of his wishes at Bologna. And it was in this city of jurisprudence, to the body of professors and students that he addressed in 1210 the collection of his decretals edited by Collivacino.

On his return to Rome, Lothar had all that a cleric needed in order to advance rapidly: acquired knowledge, family contacts, and even relationship with certain cardinals. Early he received a prebend in the chapter of St. Peter's in Rome. In 1187, Pope Gregory VIII ordained him subdeacon; in 1190, Clement III made him deacon and cardinal at the age of twenty-nine. The seat of his deaconry was the small church of Saints Sergius and Bacchus in the Roman forum between the arch of Septimus Severus and the Capitol. From there, until the end of the pontificate of Celestine III, Lothar of Segni led the busy life of all the cardinals, occupied with the reconstruction and embellishing of his diaconal church, preserving, amid the intrigues of the curia, an attitude of moderation and habits of disinterest whereby his ambition was well served.

But the brilliant student of Paris proceeded to give the world proof of his success in school. He composed his three most important treatises before his accession to the papacy.

We lack the courage to read them entirely; the feeling of deception is strong. The ordinary method of the scholastic, the accumulation of texts of Holy Scripture or the Fathers, surpasses all limits here: an ocean of citations, where at long intervals some phrases that express the thought or personal judgment of the author float on the surface. In the writings of Innocent III, treatises or sermons, one finds almost nothing of Innocent III.

Christian pessimism views the world as ugly and belittles it in order to abase man's pride. It has inspired the most celebrated of these opuscula, the *De contemptu mundi* [On the contempt of the world] or *De miseria conditionis humanae* [On the misery of the human condition], a work which had an extraordinary vogue, for we find numerous copies in all the European libraries. The cardinal said modestly in his dedication that if one recognized some merit in it, he must attribute it to the grace of God. The merit consists in carvings out of the Old and New Testaments joined together by some common ties.

This treatise opens with a description of physical illness at various ages of life. All the deformities, unhappiness, and sufferings of mankind are here accumulated and exaggerated in a truly curious way. The infant, for example, conceived in filth and blood, made of the vilest matter; what does one think of this little nude being, whimpering, weak, without defense, with an intelligence little different from that of an animal? He is inferior even to the animals, "for, after all," writes the cardinal, "when beasts are born, they walk immediately, while we, made to have rights, are not able even to go on four feet." And the sorrows of infancy, and the cries of the miserable newly-born! Lothar informs us in passing that the boy cries *A,* the girl *E,* and that the word Eve is only a double exclamation, *Heu Ha.* What is the first covering of our nakedness? A bloody film of skin! How is man, born under such conditions, above other created beings? "The vegetables produce flowers and fruits; but you, O man, what do you bring forth? Some worms, some spit, some dung."

He has spoken in the same way of the discomforts of old age, the vanity of knowledge and human occupations, the shortness of life, the misery of poor and rich, of serf and master, of celibacy and marriage. As an exception, Lothar has depicted the married woman with a rather lively touch, her eccentricities, her caprices, her love of dress, and her contrariness. "What a misfortune," he concludes, "that one never knows to what one binds himself when he marries! A horse, an ass, a cow, a dog, a cloak, a bed, a glass, a pot, all these objects we try before we buy, save for a young woman! If one shows her to her suitor, it is difficult to determine whether she displeases him; and whatever she becomes later, once the marriage is over, it is for life." In short, man is ever tormented; when he is young, by nightmares, when old, by cares, reverses of fortune, and illness. A list of the more serious illnesses leads the author to remark that men are no longer healthy and that their nature has deteriorated. Finally, to leave us in a yet more somber mood, he enumerates the diverse punishments human cruelty has invented and ends with the lugubrious history, borrowed from Josephus, of a mother who devoured her baby.

In the second book, moral evil appears as the result of three principal vices in men: cupidity, sensuality, ambition. Beside some barely-outlined portraits, of the drunkard, the *parvenu,* the proud man, that of the intriguer or pusher stands out: the cardinal must have seen this type frequently. In the chapter on luxury the clergy are taken to task with the crudity of expression proper to moralists of this period. A final book, very short, of a strict theology with little originality, demonstrates the eternity of the pains of hell and the irrevocable condemnation of the damned.

Exercise of a scholar, this is the work of a theoretician newly sharpened by scholasticism. It is not the work of a man who knew from experience the realities of life. And the historians who have vaunted it as the last word on the asceticism of the Middle Ages have been duped by an illusion. In his preface Lothar declares he is ready, on request, to develop the contrary thesis. "I will show, by the grace of God, the grandeur of the human condition so that if, by the present work, the proud man is beaten down, by its successor the humble will be exalted." Has he written this counterpart? In any case, we possess no more than the pessimistic thesis, pressed so far to the black side that, if it were necessary to take the quibbles of this Roman prelate seriously, nothing would be left of the justice and bounty of the divine being.

The two other treatises, *The Sacred Mystery of the Altar* and *The Four Kinds of Marriage,* are only applications of mystical symbolism dear to the theologians of this period. In these Lothar compares the unions represented in Christ and his Church, in God and the love of the just, in the Word and human nature, in carnal marriage and a legitimate wife. He poses and resolves some strange problems, among others "whether Christ ought to be called a bigamist." Here he interprets by symbols all the elements of the sacrifice of the mass: words, deeds, and movements of the priest, priestly vestments and the accessories of the cult. Allegory is everywhere, even in the miter of the bishop. The two horns are the two testaments; the two little bands at the fringe, the spirit and the letter. The crosier, sign of the power of correction possessed by the bishop, has a pointed tip to goad the lazy; its stem is straight because the bishop has the duty to reprimand the weak; it is curved at the top because he is charged with gathering in errant souls.

These works of the young Innocent III in no way announce the political genius and the firmness of spirit of one of the greatest popes of the Middle Ages. But contemporaries did not judge them as we do. They were pleased with this rhetoric and enraptured before these subtle puerilities. We must indeed believe, since they said it, that the prestige of Lothar of Segni as theologian, moralist, and writer had a bearing on his accession.

*   *   *

About Christmas, 1197, Pope Celestine III, a nonagenarian, fell ill, and the approach of the end redoubled the agitation of the cardinals. The youngest of them, Lothar, was the foremost; for a long time a devoted party had supported him. This is perhaps the reason why Celestine decided to seek another successor. The old do not like to be replaced by one too young, and besides, he was a member of the Orsini family, an enemy of Lothar's family. He immediately began to prepare the way for the cardinal of St. Prisca, a Colonna. He made him a coadjutor, insinuating that he would abdicate voluntarily if someone promised to name his candidate.

In all periods there have been popes who, for family interests or to avoid a schism, have tried to choose their own successor. All established power looks to its perpetuation either by heredity proper or by prior designation. But the cardinals unanimously repulsed a combination that would annul their electoral right. The opinion of the church, little favorable to practices of this kind, refused to abase the character of the highest religious office. The recommendations that Celestine III made at his death to his entourage met with no success.

The candidates were numerous. "The Lord Cardinal Bishop of Ostia," said a contemporary, the chronicler Richard of Hovedon, "worked to become pope himself, as well as the Cardinal Bishop of Porto and Lord Jordan of Fossanova and Master Gratian. And all the other cardinals attempted, each on his own account, to reach the same goal." The Englishman could indeed make fun of the court of Rome. Celestine III died on January 8, 1198, and on the same day, in spite of the abundance of candidates, he was replaced.

The election was held in a Roman ruin that the Middle Ages had transformed into a fortress, the Septizonium, the debris of a magnificent three-storied monument built by Septimius Severus on the southeast of the Palatine between the Circus Maximus and the Colosseum. It belonged to the monks of St. Andrew, possessors of the Coelian hill, and its name occurred often in the annals of medieval Rome. It was there that the nephew of Gregory VII had defended himself against Henry IV, that Pascal II had escaped the pursuit of the Germans, and that Victor III had been elected. One could deliberate there without fear. When Lothar and part of his colleagues had concluded the funeral at the Lateran, they hastened to rejoin the rest of the conclave enclosed in the Septizonium, and the decisive operation began.

After the mass of the Holy Spirit, the cardinals prostrated themselves and then gave each other the kiss of peace. They named the tellers who would collect the written ballots and read the tally. Lothar obtained the greatest number of votes; Cardinal John of Salerno had ten; two other cardinals divided the rest. They then discussed the outcome. The problem was Lothar's age: to elect the youngest member of the curia! to choose a thirty-seven-year-old pope! But this candidate was learned, of irreproachable morals, and finally, the impelling reason was that the situation of the Church demanded an active, vigorous, and militant head. The electors therefore agreed on the name of Lothar of Segni. John of Salerno himself rallied to the choice of the majority and the final vote was unanimous.

Following a tradition of ecclesiastical humility which emphasized the distressing side of the task to be fulfilled, the elect refused at first the honor they wished to bestow on him: "he wept and sobbed," then he gave in. The eldest of the cardinal-deacons put the purple mantle on his shoulders and gave him the name Innocent III. Two cardinal-bishops led him to the altar where he prayed face down, while the cantors and the whole college intoned the *Te Deum*. He then sat down behind the altar, and the cardinals came there in rotation to kiss his foot and his lips. The first phase of the accession, the election, was ended.

Could such an important event in the

history of the Middle Ages as the exaltation of Innocent III occur without a sign from the divine will? Three doves flew into the hall of the conclave: one of these birds, of immaculate whiteness, settled at his right and did not stir. In addition, the elect had a vision. He had been told that he would marry his mother, *i.e.*, the Roman Church. Other revelations on this subject were made to pious personages, but we shall pass over them in silence, for Innocent himself did not want them talked about.

For more than a century, the lower clergy and people of Rome had not taken part in the election, which was the responsibility of the cardinals alone. But they were far from being uninterested. A crowd of clerics and laymen awaited the result of the voting outside the Septizonium. When it was announced, they escorted the elect, in acclamation, to the basilica of St. John Lateran where he would be enthroned.

The palace of the Lateran, contiguous to the sanctuary, was the seat of papal government, the center of the Christian world. It occupied the largest part of the square of St. John, from which, as seen today, the view embraces the red line of the ancient walls, the ruined aqueducts, and, in the background, the violet slopes of the Alban hills prominent against the snow of the Sabines. Two groups of buildings contained, on the west, the great council hall supported on its demi-turrets; on the east, the private apartments of the popes, the dining-room of Leo III, where public banquets were given, the oratories of St. Sylvester and St. Lawrence, the chapel, and the chancery. The palace disappeared in the time of Sixtus V [1585–1590], but the basilica of St. John still remains, though renovated, with its ancient baptistry and its cloister; it was before the portico that was then in front of the church that the new pope was immediately presented to the Roman people.

The cardinals installed Innocent III on a sculpted marble seat, the *sedes stercoraria,* the throne of dung, used because of the verse in Scripture: "He has caused the poor man to arise from dirt and dung so that he sits with princes on the throne of glory." The chamberlain who remained at the pope's side gave him three handfuls of pennies, and he threw them to the crowd massed in the square, saying: "Gold and silver are not for my pleasure; what I have, I give you." When that was done, he was greeted by a new acclamation: "St. Peter has chosen the Lord Innocent." Followed by the prior and canons of St. John Lateran, he entered the church and went to sit on the papal throne behind the altar. Then he mounted the great interior stairway which led from the basilica to the chapel of St. Sylvester, where other ceremonies awaited him.

Two red marble curule thrones were there. Innocent first sat in the one on the right. The prior of St. Lawrence, head of the chapel clergy, put a scepter in his hand, as well as the keys of the church and the palace, signs of his authority over the personnel and of possession of even the property itself. The new master then sat on the throne on the left and the prior passed a cincture of red silk, from which a scarlet purse hung, around his body. It contained twelve seals of precious material and a bag of musk. By this Innocent was given the papal treasure and some objects of value it contained. Then the officials of the palace were presented and permitted to kiss him. Again he threw pieces of money to those assisting with these words: "He has thrown away his treasures, he has distributed them to the poor, and his justice will endure forever." Finally they led the pope from the chapel of St. Sylvester to the oratory of St. Lawrence or the Sancta Sanctorum [Holy of Holies], the only part of the ancient palace preserved today. Innocent prayed there before a special altar; then he entered his private apartments.

The essentials were over. After the ceremonies at the Septizonium and the Lateran, the pope, elected and installed, held power legally. The consecration remained, but it was not necessary for this third act of the accession to follow the other two immediately. Since Innocent was only a deacon, it was necessary to ordain him to the priesthood before consecrating him bishop. The ordination took place on February 21, 1198, six weeks after the election, and on the following Sunday, the feast of St. Peter's Chair, he was consecrated in the basilica of the Vatican.

Protected by the fortified walls of the Leonine city for which the Castello di Sant'Angelo served as an advance bastion, the famous Church of St. Peter offered as a first view its campanile and the triple entrance of its portico. Here, as at the Lateran, the sanctuary lay beyond an atrium, a vast interior court where pilgrims stopped before the tomb of the Emperor Otto II and drank at the huge fir cone in gilded bronze, the *pigna,* from which water poured profusely between eight columns of porphyry. Next the façade of the basilica came into view, with its windows, its five doors, and the immense mosaic which showed Christ seated between St. Peter and the Virgin, the Evangelists and their symbolic animals. Inside, five aisles ended, as in most Roman churches, in a straight transept and a semi-circular apse. At the back of the apse was the throne of St. Peter; in the middle of the transept, the *Confession,* an inestimable treasure. The whole world knew its mosaics of gold, its altar of silver, its gilded canopy with four twisted columns of oriental alabaster. Just below the *Confession* a shaft communicated with the funerary chamber where a constant tradition placed the bones of the Apostle. It was there especially that the crowd pressed, but they also besieged the numerous chapels open at the sides. The main aisle, finally, as the curious miniature of the French painter, John Fouquet, shows it, had an imposing character, with its double range of antique columns and the elegant balustrade on its circumference. A small square chapel occupied the extreme left.

It was into this chapel, on February 22, 1198, that Innocent III was led by the canons of the basilica to put on ceremonial sandals and to vest in the papal robes. Then, passing behind the main altar, he sat at the foot of the steps that led to the throne of St. Peter. The bishops and cardinals, according to ritual, formed a circle around him. The consecrator, the Bishop of Ostia, put the gospels on his head and all, without saying a word, extended their right hands to him. After the ceremony of anointing, they gave him the ring and the pallium; they put the gospels into his hands. Then he arose and was put on the throne of the Apostle. At this moment, at the chant of *Gloria in excelsis,* began the procession of assistants, who rendered the customary homage to him.

Remaining seated, Innocent watched the deacons, the secretaries, and papal judges, vested in red mantles, divide into two groups. The one sang: "Hear, O Christ!" The other responded: "Long life to our Lord Innocent, Sovereign Pontiff and Universal Pope." And the dialogue continued: "Savior of the world!" — "Come to his aid." And the one side invoked the series of great Roman saints: Gabriel, Raphael, John the Baptist, Peter, Paul, Andrew, Stephen, Leo, Gregory, Benedict, Basil, Saba, Agnes, Cecilia, Lucy. To each name the one choir pronounced, the other responded: "Come to his aid." A *Kyrie eleison,* chanted in unison by the two groups, closed the solemnities.

When the pope had said mass, preached, gone to communion, and blessed the faithful, he went out to the entrance of the basilica surrounded by a crowd of clergy. There, in view of the Romans singing the *Kyrie eleison,* the first of the cardinal-deacons raised over him the episcopal miter and tiara, the royal power. From that time he was vested with political dominion over the churches and their peoples.

Then the great procession was organized and began to move. The pope and his clergy had to go by way of the "Triumphal Road" from St. Peter's of Rome to St. John Lateran. At the head of the cortege was the magnificently adorned

ceremonial horse of the pontiff. A subdeacon carried the cross. Twelve officers
of the militia with red banners and two
others with lances surmounted by gilded
cherubim [followed]. Then [came] the
maritime prefects, the notaries, lawyers,
judges, choir, abbots from outside Rome,
bishops, archbishops, the Roman abbots,
the cardinal-priests, the cardinal-deacons.
Finally, the pope himself appeared,
mounted on a horse with a scarlet saddle-
cloth. A valet carried an umbrella over his
head. At his sides rode the two most nota-
ble personages of Rome, the senator and
the prefect of the city, followed by the
nobility and representatives of the Italian
cities, friends or subjects of the papacy.

The cavalcade crossed the Tiber at the
bridge of Nero. It stopped at the palace of
Maximus in the Campo dei Fiori, then
dominated by a fortress, and at the church
of St. Mark. Passing the ruins of the imperial fora, it stopped again at the church
of St. Adrian, then entered the Roman
forum, which it crossed lengthwise in the
direction of the Via Sacra. It passed to the
north of the Colosseum, skirted the church
of St. Lawrence and finally arrived at the
pontifical palace by the Via San Giovanni
in Laterano. On the whole route, the cor-
porations (the *scholae*) or rich individuals
had erected arches of greenery. At each
street corner, the clergy of the Roman
parishes had gathered, incense-burners in
their hands. An enormous crowd, bearing
palms and flowers, singing and shooting
arrows, acclaimed the sovereign as he
passed.

But he had to pay for his welcome.
Money played a large part in this triumph.
At certain places on the way, the papal
servants threw small sums of money to the
people. For each of the arches under which
the procession passed, for each of the
groups of clergy who flowed into the
crossroads, a duty was paid and the amount
inscribed in the book of Cardinal Cencio,
a ritual repeated by a financial secretary.
Even the Jews of Rome, come down to the

foot of the Campo dei Fiori, offered the
pope the book of the law and received a
present of money. Each of the major and
minor officials of the curia had the right
to a meal, to a small sum, to a provision
of bread and meat. Even the lay authorities of Rome, Senator, prefect, judges,
claimed their part of the food and money.

When he had returned to the palace,
Innocent sat once more in the oratory of
St. Sylvester and all the prelates came, one
after another, to genuflect before him. A
surpliced chamberlain, assisted by a clerk
of the chamber and two bankers of the city,
stood before a large table covered with piles
of money and handed the pope, in a cup
of silver, the amount due each personage.
That night, there was a ceremonial ban-
quet in the great dining-room of Leo III,
decorated with mosaics, paved with marble,
cooled by the stream of water from an
enormous porphyry fountain. The table
of the pope, higher than the others, spar-
kling with gold and silver vases, was served
by the eldest and noblest of the lay assistants. At the table to the right, the cardinal-
bishops and priests were seated; at that
on the left, the cardinal-deacons. Farther
away, the bishops and nobles of the city
sat.

We would like to know the attitude of
Innocent III to these ceremonies and feasts.
History furnishes only a detail. At the
moment of his anointing, "he had such a
contrite heart that he shed abundant tears."
Perhaps this too was a tradition.

*   *   *

It was an established custom for the new
pontiff himself to announce his accession
to the churches and princes of Christendom. Innocent had the greater reason to
follow the custom because he had to explain his accession to the papal throne at
the age of thirty-seven. An encyclical, dated
the very day after his election, announced
to Europe, therefore, what had happened
the day before at the Septizonium. The
pope did not speak of the first ballot, which

had brought only a majority of votes to his name; he devoted himself to the rallying ballot, which was unanimous for him.

"All have turned their eyes on us, insufficient as we are, mindful, perhaps, that it was Benjamin who found the cup of money at the bottom of the sack. Several, however, were by age, by position, and by merit more worthy than we of such an honor. Convinced of our lack of ability, we at first refused this office, so heavy for our weak shoulders; but we had to surrender to the insistence of our brethren. In prolonging resistance we could have opened the door to a dangerous schism or appeared to oppose the decrees of the divine will." But why the preference shown for the youngest? He himself did not explain it well: "The ways of God are mysterious and his judgments incomprehensible. And it is not without surprise that we sometimes see the young man come before the old in the exercise of the highest authority." In his letter to the Patriarch of Jerusalem, he insists once more, with good nature, on the unanimity of the vote and remarks that the cardinals, contrary to rule, held the election on the same day as the funeral of his predecessor.

Despite the formulae of official modesty, Lothar of Segni, after having reached the highest goal the ambition of man could then seek, believed that he was ready to bear the enormous burden. He wanted to take charge with full knowledge of his duties and his rights. Scarcely was he enthroned than he seized the opportunity to tell the Roman people and the whole Church what he thought of his office and the authority it conferred on him.

The sermon he preached on the day of his consecration permitted him to justify the pre-eminence of papal power. In his view, it was based on the superiority of the Apostle Peter attested by the *Tu es Petrus* ["Thou art Peter, and upon this rock I will build my church. . . ." Matthew xvi, 18] and the gospel account of the barque of the Apostle. Without doubt, to remain faithful to the duty of humility the Church prescribed for its members, Innocent called himself the servant of the servants of God and dwelt on the obligations rather than on the advantages of his office. But in the same phrase where he spoke of his personal unworthiness, he defined, with a kind of transport of pride, the immense extent of the papal power: "Who am I myself or what was the house of my father that I am permitted to sit above kings, to possess the throne of glory? For it is to me that the words of the prophet apply: 'I have placed you above peoples and kingdoms that you may uproot and destroy as well as build and plant.' It is to me that he has said: 'I will give you the keys of the kingdom of heaven and what you will loose on earth will be loosed in heaven.'" See therefore what kind of servant he is who commands the whole family. He is the Vicar of Jesus Christ, the Successor of Peter . . . he is the mediator between God and man, less than God but greater than man.

When he celebrated the anniversary of his accession the next year, he treated the same subject again in a different way. He was the spouse of the Roman Church and the Bishop of Rome has no superior but God himself. But what is the explanation (here the spirit of scholasticism reappears) for the fact that the spouse of the Roman Church is in charge of the other churches? Is it not contrary to the laws of marriage, which prohibit more than one wife? To this objection, he answered that, in fact, certain bishops have two churches, *e.g.*, the Bishop of Ostia, who is at the same time Bishop of Velletri. And besides, the Roman Church has the right to do with the pope what Sarah in the Bible did, who led Agar to the bed of her husband Abraham. Rome brought to the pope all of the other churches, its servants. Innocent perceived, however, that he was spending a little too much time on this scholastic argument. "You who are interested in these problems look for the reasons to justify this apparent violation of the laws of marriage; for my-self, my other cares do not leave me the time." But the love of symbolism drove him further: "The Roman Church, which I have espoused, did not have empty hands; she brought me a dowry: the fullness of spiritual power and vast temporal posses-sions. For the Apostle Peter alone is the one who has been called to enjoy the dual authority. I have received from Rome the miter, sign of my religious office, and the tiara, which confers terrestrial dominion on me."

This idea is often expressed in the ser-mons of Innocent III. For him, Rome has always occupied and will occupy for-ever the first rank in the universe. It rules over bodies as over souls. At other times, it possessed only the temporal power; it joined to that the spiritual authority. "It held both the keys of heaven and the government of earth."

Make no mistake about the Pope's thought: he believed that Rome, with its dual power, with its double character of "Apostolic" and imperial town, was his. And when he spoke of empire, he did not think of the German sovereign. He was at the same time pope and emperor. He stated this in positive terms in the sermon he delivered on the Feast of Pope Sylvester. Then, the question was no longer merely one of the superiority of the Apostle Peter; the papal power was based on an actual event which had taken place several cen-turies before. Like all his predecessors In-nocent adapted to his use the famous legend of the Donation of Constantine. "This excellent emperor learned by a heavenly revelation that Pope Sylvester had, at his baptism, delivered him from leprosy. When he was established at Byzantium, he took for himself the Eastern Empire and gave the pope at Rome the senate and the whole Western Empire. He even wanted to put his own crown on the pope's head, but Sylvester refused, con-tented to wear as a diadem the royal head-dress circled with gold. In virtue of his religious authority, the pope named patri-archs, primates, metropolitans, and bishops; in virtue of his kingly power, the senators, prefects, judges, and notaries. As king he wore the tiara, as chief bishop, the miter. He used the miter on all occasions; he used the tiara less because the spiritual authority was more ancient, higher, and more ex-tensive than the royal authority. Among the people of God, the priesthood surpassed the empire."

From this very clear teaching proceeded the whole history of Innocent's pontificate. One finds there the essential thread of his doctrine and his deeds. The power he held was at the same time evangelical and historical, by nature spiritual and temporal. Without doubt, like all great clerics of the Middle Ages, he believed that the religious power was very superior to the other; but he would use both, and as both seemed to him legitimate, he would devote his life to strengthening both.

Enunciated from the lofty throne at the Vatican and the Lateran, these principles were proclaimed with tremendous force in the correspondence Innocent carried on with the clergy and sovereigns of Europe. It is enough to peruse the letters of the first year of his rule to be struck by the number of passages where there is a ques-tion of the nature and extent of papal power. On each page we find statements like this one: "We are placed by God above peoples and kingdoms. . . . We hold the place of Christ on earth, and, by his example, we have the duty and the desire to bring peace to men. . . . Seated on the throne of dignity, we judge in justice even the kings themselves. . . . Nothing that happens in the universe ought to escape the attention and control of the sovereign pontiff." Writing to the clergy of France to announce the arrival of their legate, he excused himself for not being able to be everywhere. But human nature had its limits and forced him to have recourse to his brethren. He seemed to regret it: "If the interest of the Church would permit it, I would like best to do everything for myself." This depicts the man and the enormous need for activity he desired to satisfy during the eighteen years of his pontificate.

Two of the letters from the year 1198 attract special attention. In a letter to the Archbishop of Monreale, Innocent demonstrated once again the thesis of the pre-eminence of the Apostle Peter, *i.e.*, of the supremacy of the Roman Church and he stated the view, historically false, that Peter and his successors had established archbishops and bishops throughout the whole world and divided the Christian world into provinces and dioceses. The letter to the Rectors of Tuscany began with a comparison still famous: "God, creator of the world, has put two great stars in the firmament to enlighten it: the sun which presides over the day, the moon which commands the night. Likewise, he has instituted two high dignitaries in the firmament of the universal Church: the papacy, which reigns over souls, and the royalty, which rules bodies. As the moon receives its light from the sun, which is so much more important because of the amount and quality of its light, so the royal power draws all its luster and prestige from the papal power. But the two supremacies, the two powers, have their seat in Italy. Italy, by a decree of Providence, possesses, therefore, superiority over all the lands of the earth. The font of the Christian religion is in Italy and, in the primacy of the Apostolic See, the authority of the empire and the priesthood are intertwined." Here again, Innocent seems to ignore the Germanic Empire and its pretensions to dominion over the world.

That this man took pride in his title and wished to push to the extreme limit the exercise of his rights, of his religious and terrestrial authority, there can be no doubt, and he himself did not conceal it. Elsewhere, he moderated the very real expression of this intoxication with power by the formulae demanded by priestly humility.

His pen was not sparing of the words "unworthiness" and "insufficiency." In ending his sermon on the apostolic primacy, he said to the faithful gathered at St. Peter's in Rome: "Lift up your pure hands to heaven and ask God in your prayer to make me fulfill worthily this office of pontifical servitude under which my shoulders bow; that He permit me to act for the glory of His name, for the salvation of my soul, for the profit of the church, and the good of all Christian people."

His office of judge and statesman absorbed him, crushed him. He did not cease to complain in his correspondence as in each of the prefaces to his theological treatises: "I am devoured utterly in the abyss of my many occupations and of the cares the government of the world causes me. It is above human resources. . . . Caught up in the infinite network of affairs," he wrote elsewhere, "I am so divided that I find myself inevitably inferior to each of my tasks. They do not leave me time to meditate, scarcely to breathe. A servant to the interests of others, I belong no more to myself. Nevertheless, so as not to neglect the care of God's affairs, so that no one can say that I permit myself to be monopolized by earthly matters with which the misfortunes of the times crush me, I have drawn up these sermons."

A significant admission. Innocent III recognized that he was obliged to neglect the spiritual for the temporal, and he laid the fault on the wickedness of men. He reproached himself, evidently, for being embroiled thus in the whirlwind of the age. Addressing himself to the Abbot and religious of Citeaux, he implored the monks to intercede for him before God. "Your holy prayers will give me the strength that I lack. He who aided the Apostle Peter at the moment of his shipwreck will restore me, too, to the road of salvation; He will prevent me from being plunged, more than necessary, into the vanities of life."

This was not a banal formula, but the sincere expression of a justified scruple. Elsewhere, the new pope lost no time in debating with his conscience. From the day following his election, we see him acting everywhere at once with a decision and vigor of which the papacy had seemed incapable.

THE VICAR OF CHRIST

If Innocent claimed temporal authority, on what did he base this claim? In the opinion of A. J. and R. W. Carlyle, a view in which C. H. McIlwain largely concurs, Innocent based his claim to exercise temporal authority on his position as Vicar of Christ. Alexander (1861–1943) and Robert (1859–1934) Carlyle were educated at Glasgow and Cambridge. They devoted a large part of their scholarly effort to the production of their *Mediaeval Political Theory in the West.* C. H. McIlwain (b. 1871) established an international reputation in political thought while he was teaching at Harvard. His writings have covered almost the entire sweep in the history of political theory.

Judged by God Alone

A. J. AND R. W. CARLYLE

THE compiler of the Decretals did not hesitate to include very strong statements regarding the powers and pre-eminence of the Popes; these do not, however, give a complete idea of Innocent's claims. So far as they go we have shown, in discussing the relevant passages, that while Innocent held that the spiritual power was greatly superior in dignity to the temporal, yet he also held that both alike were of divine appointment. In the case of the empire Innocent admitted the right of the German princes to elect their king to be promoted to the empire, after his coronation by the Pope, but he claimed the right and authority to examine the person elected and to decide whether he was fit for empire. He also claimed the right to decide in the case of disputed elections. In the case of disputes between rulers, Innocent claimed the right to arbitrate where a question of sin was involved.

In the Vercelli case he laid down the rule that suitors would not be heard by the Holy See in matters within the jurisdiction of the secular courts, unless justice were refused by the civil authorities concerned. Should justice be refused, recourse might be had to the bishop or to the Pope; especially at a time when the empire was vacant and there was no superior to whom they might appeal for justice. Finally, it seems that he maintained that it was for the Pope to decide in cases where it was uncertain whether the matter was one for ecclesiastical or for secular authorities to deal with. The passages cited in the Decretals, from Innocent, do not include any reference to Constantine's donation, but there is an important statement on this subject in one of his sermons to which we shall refer later on.

Every reader of Innocent's letters must be struck by his tremendous assertion of the Pope's exalted position. Gregory VII was content to be the vicar of St. Peter. For Innocent, the Pope is the vicar of Christ (or sometimes of God); less than

From A. J. and R. W. Carlyle, *Mediaeval Political Theory in the West,* V (Edinburgh: Wm. Blackwood & Sons, 1903), 151–86. By permission of the publisher.

God but greater than man; the successor of Peter and vested with the same powers. Thus in a sermon on the consecration of the Pope (possibly the sermon preached by him on the day of his own consecration) he speaks of himself as placed above all peoples and kingdoms, endowed with the fulness of power, less than God but greater than man, judging all, but judged by God alone. In another sermon on the anniversary of his consecration he speaks of his marriage to the Church (of Rome) and of the dowry he has received — a priceless dowry, the fulness of spiritual and the "latitudo" of temporal powers. As a sign thereof he has received the mitre to indicate his spiritual and the crown to indicate his temporal power. His authority is divine rather than human. He has received of God such fulness of spiritual power that no increase thereof is possible. Innocent complained in March 1211 to the Archbishop of Ravenna of the behaviour of Otto IV. From his letter it appears that many held that he had brought his sufferings on his own head by raising Otto to the throne. His reply was that God Himself said He repented having created man. As there is no acceptance of persons with God, so there can be none with him. He has been exalted to a throne where he judges even princes, and should the King of France, trusting in his might, oppose the Pope's commands, he will be unable to stand before the face of God, of whom the Pope is viceregent. Innocent compares the despatch of his envoys to the faithful, to the missions entrusted by Christ to his disciples. He cannot tolerate contempt shown to himself, nay, rather to God whose place he holds on earth. Philip (of France) should recognize what honour and glory he had received from all Christians for his obedience to the Pope's orders. Kings so revere him that they hold devoted service to him to be a condition of good government. Injured persons may have recourse to the Pope, the highest authority, and bound to do justice as "debtor both to the wise and to the unwise." The Arch-

bishop of Tours is commended for consulting the Pope about matters regarding which he was in doubt, as the Apostolic See has by divine ordinance been placed over the whole world, and should be referred to by all in doubt on any matter. The King of Armenia is praised because he sought the help of the Roman Church, not only in spiritual but also in temporal matters, and because he appealed to it to help him in defending his just claims (in justitiis suis). The name of the Apostolic See is revered even among nations which do not know God. God who "wrought effectually in Peter to the apostleship," also "wrought effectually" through Innocent, persuading Philip by means of the papal legate to make a truce with Richard. He writes to Richard of England that he has taken action after consulting with the cardinals, and in accordance with divine revelation (divinitus revelatum). The pre-eminence of the Apostolic See is due, not to the decree of any synod but to divine ordinance. There proceeds from the Apostolic See a sword, very sharp and swift, and it binds those whom it strikes, not on earth alone but also in heaven.

It is as the successors of Peter that Innocent claims for the Popes their exalted position. In virtue of this succession they are vicars of Christ, and as his vicars they have received from him authority (principatum et magisterium) over all Churches, over all clerics, nay more, over all the faithful. Others have limited rule, the Pope alone has the fulness of power. While the Popes are inferior to Peter in sanctity and in the power of working miracles, they are in every respect his equals so far as their jurisdiction is concerned. It is from St. Peter that the Apostolic See (or as Innocent also calls it the Roman Church, or the Universal Church) has received the primacy over all other Churches. James, the brother of our Lord, content with Jerusalem, left to Peter the government not only of the Church Universal, but also of the whole world (sæculum).

We must now examine what authority

Innocent did claim as Pope in temporal matters. In a previous volume we have seen that in one of his letters he compared the pontifical and the royal authority to the sun and moon. In another letter he developed this. As the moon receives its light from the sun, so the splendour of the royal power and authority is derived from the pontifical authority. The logical conclusion would appear to be that the royal authority is derived from the pontifical. Innocent, however, did not draw the conclusion, though here as in other cases he appears, consciously or unconsciously, to be laying a foundation for future explicit claims. It is clear from other letters that Innocent did not as Pope claim supreme temporal power. Thus, in a letter to the consul and people of Jesi, he speaks of his unlimited spiritual jurisdiction over peoples and kingdoms, while by the grace of God he has also much power in temporal matters. Again, in a letter to the Archbishop of Ravenna, he writes, that ecclesiastical liberty is nowhere better secured than where the Roman Church has authority both in temporal and in spiritual matters. In the Government of the Ecclesia two swords are required, the spiritual and the material. Both are given by God direct; the one to spiritual and the other to temporal rulers. We shall deal later on with Innocent's reference to Constantine's donation; we need only mention here that he treats the donation by the emperor as of grace, and there is no suggestion, as in Innocent IV's letters, that the Pope only received from Constantine that to which he was already entitled.

We have still, however, to explain Innocent's explicit assertion of Peter's supremacy, not only over the whole Church, but also over the whole "sæculum" or "mundum." It was in virtue of his office as Christ's vicar, in succession to Peter, that he appointed and deposed kings, that he gave them protection, that he ordered contending parties to make peace, that he took the orphans and widows of crusaders under his protection, and that he confirmed treaties of peace, agreements, grants, and statutes. We shall give some examples of the action taken by him in various cases, and the grounds given by him for taking it.

Towards the end of 1199 or the beginning of 1200 Innocent had written Kaloyan of Bulgaria (whom he addressed simply as "nobilis") asking him to receive his legate. Kaloyan did not reply till 1202. In his letter Kaloyan, who styled himself emperor, asked the Church of Rome to grant him a crown and the honours given to his ancestors. Innocent replied on the 27th November 1202, addressing Kaloyan this time as "dominus" of the Bulgarians and Wallachians, informing him that he found in the papal registers that many kings, of the lands now subject to him, had been crowned, and that his chaplain whom he was sending to Bulgaria would, among other matters, inquire into the facts regarding the crown conferred by the Church of Rome on his ancestors.

As Bulgaria had only regained its independence from the Greek Empire a few years before, and the fourth crusade had just commenced, caution was obviously necessary in formally recognizing the Bulgarian kingdom. In the following year, after the capture of Constantinople in July and the restoration of the emperor Isaac Angelus to the throne, the situation had altered. Some time before September, 1203, Kaloyan wrote Innocent telling him that the Greeks had sent him their patriarch, promising to crown him as emperor, and to make his archbishop a patriarch (Innocent had not done so), but he refused their advances and again asked the Pope to have him crowned as emperor and to promote his archbishop. Innocent replied holding out to the "dominus Bulgarorum" hopes that his requests would be granted. A few months later the Pope wrote Kaloyan, "the King of the Bulgarians and Wallachians," that he was sending him by a cardinal, a sceptre and a diadem. In virtue of his power as vicar of Christ, and bound to feed his sheep, he appointed him king over his flock, trusting in the authority of him by whom Samuel anointed David as king, and seeking to provide for the welfare of the people both spiritually and temporally. Before his legate crowned him, Kaloyan was to swear that he and his successors, and all the lands and peoples subject to him, would remain devoted and obedient to the Roman Church. As requested by Kaloyan's envoy, he gave the king authority to mint money with his image on it (tuo charactere insignitum). There is no reference in this letter to the previous history of Bulgaria, nor to the inquiries previously ordered by Innocent, the action is based solely on Innocent's authority as vicar of Christ. In a separate letter, probably written at the same time, he sent the king a standard (vexillum) to "use against those who honour the crucified one with their lips, but whose heart is far from him."

Sverre, the King of Norway, had for some time been engaged in a serious conflict with the Church in Norway, and Innocent directed that his followers should be excommunicated and their lands placed under interdict. He also ordered the King of Denmark (per apostolica scripta mandamus) to take up arms against him. He also directed the Archbishop of Norway to excommunicate a bishop supporting him. This was in 1198. In 1211, long after Sverre's death, the disputed succession again came before Innocent, the supporters of his descendants still refusing to accept the Pope as arbiter.

Besides appointing and deposing kings, we find Innocent actively supporting them. Thus in March 1202, before John's final breach with Philip, Innocent wrote the Archbishop of Rouen, directing him to take action against John's rebellious barons in Normandy, or in his other lands in France. He was, on the Pope's authority, to warn them, and if this failed he was to inflict ecclesiastical punishments.

We may take other instances of Innocent's action in protecting kings from his dealings with Hungary. It is noticeable that, though the Roman Church had long-standing claims on Hungary as a feudal State, the Pope does not issue any of his orders as feudal lord of the kingdom. Bela, King of Hungary, was succeeded by his son Emerich, who had been crowned during his father's lifetime. Coelestine III forbade the Hungarians to assist Andrew, Emerich's brother, on pain of excommunication, and in support of this policy one of the first letters written by Innocent after his accession was to the Abbot of St. Martin's, summoning him to Rome to answer for the support he had given to Andrew. Before his consecration he also wrote Andrew, directing him to carry out the promise he had given his father to go on crusade. In case of failure he would be anathematised, and should his brother die childless he would be passed over in the succession by his younger brother. In June the same year, at Emerich's request, Innocent allowed the king, so long as Hungary was in a disturbed state, to retain in the kingdom any twenty crusaders he chose. He wrote at the same time to Andrew, ordering him (per apostolica scripta tibi mandamus) to be faithful to his brother, and forbidding him to make an armed attack on the king or to stir up sedition against him. Disobedience was to be punished by excommunication, and his lands and those of his supporters were to be placed under interdict. In February 1203 he directed the archbishops and bishops in Hungary to give an oath of fidelity to Ladislaus before his father, Emerich, started on crusade. He gave this order that the pontifical authority should so guard and defend the kingdom that it could not be transferred to another. A year later, at the king's request, he ordered the Archbishop of Gram to crown his son, though a minor; the father giving, on behalf of his son, the customary oath of obedience to the Roman Church, and an undertaking to maintain the liberty of the Hungarian Church. In April 1205, after the death of Emerich, the Pope wrote, as vicar of Christ and bound by his apostolic office to protect minors, directing Andrew not to allow the regalia to be dispersed during the minority of his nephew, Ladislaus. At the same time he directed the Hungarian clergy to defend the king against attack. In June 1206 he again addressed the Hungarian prelates and nobles on behalf of Ladislaus, directing them on pain of ecclesiastical penalties to take the oath of fidelity.

We must turn to another important aspect of Innocent's relations to the Temporal Power. We find him frequently intervening in conflicts between rulers, endeavouring to persuade or compel them to peace with each other. We shall in later chapters have to consider the similar action specially of Boniface VIII, and in our next volume we shall have to deal with some works which seem to indicate that the conception of some international system or method of setting forward peace was, for some time at least, of importance.

In a previous volume we have dealt with Innocent's letter to the French archbishops and bishops regarding his claim to arbitrate between Philip, King of France, and John, King of England, and requiring the cessation of hostilities.

There were many previous and subsequent cases in which Innocent directed the contending parties to make peace or a long truce, but this case is remarkable from the stress laid by Innocent on the fact that he was taking action on a complaint by John that Philip had sinned against him, and that he was therefore bound as Pope to deal with the complaint and to inquire into the charge. This was the letter finally selected for the Decretals, no doubt because it appeared to give the Pope all the power he required, while avoiding the appearance of direct intervention in political controversies. It would be difficult to conceive of a case in which one or both of the contending parties could not be accused of sin.

According to Wendover, a papal legate had endeavoured, in 1189, to compel Philip of France and Richard to come to terms with Richard's father, Henry II, and had threatened to put all Philip's lands under interdict. Philip refused to submit to the legate's orders, and denied that the Roman Church had any right to sentence a King of France for punishing a rebellious vassal, the very point taken by Philip in 1203. In 1198, the first year of Innocent's pontificate, Richard appears to have complained to the Pope of injuries he had received during his absence on crusade. One of the persons he accused was Philip. The Pope replied that Philip had brought counter charges, and that he hoped to be able to come himself and inquire into the matter. Should he be unable to come, he would have the matter settled by a legate. He concluded his letter by a peremptory order to Richard to make peace and to keep it; otherwise, trusting in the power of the Almighty, whose vicar he was, he would by ecclesiastical pressure (districtione) compel him and the King of France to keep the peace. He also wrote a similar letter to Philip, dwelling on the obligation that lay on himself as Pope to restore peace among those at variance with one another.

While Philip and John were at war in 1203 the Pope issued peremptory orders to Philip to make peace, or a truce with a view to a lasting peace.

He threatened Philip in case of disobedience with ecclesiastical penalties, and wrote a similar letter to John. In his letter to Philip he based his action on the duty laid on him to seek peace and ensue it. He dwelt on the horrors of war, and on the encouragement given to the Saracens by this conflict between Christians. He was bound to interfere lest the blood of the multitudes slain be required at his hand, and he therefore sent his envoys to secure peace, or a truce leading to peace, between the two kings. Philip, before answering, called a meeting of his magnates, ecclesiastical and lay. After he was assured of their support, he replied, according to a papal letter, that he was not bound to submit to the papal decision in feudal matters (de jure feodi et hominii), and that the Pope had no say in controversies between kings (nihil ad nos (*i.e.*, the Pope) pertinet de negotio quod vertitur inter reges). Innocent, in his reply, expressed his astonishment that the king should appear to wish to limit the Pope's jurisdiction in matters. He expressly disclaimed any intention of dealing with a feudal matter, but with the question of sin, raised by John's complaints against Philip. This is the first letter in which the Pope refers to these complaints. He still dwells in this letter on the evils and wickedness of war. This was on the 31st October 1203. A few months later, probably in April 1204, Innocent wrote the French ecclesiastics a letter, portions of which were incorporated in the Decretals, and to which we have previously referred. In this letter the Pope lays much more stress than in his letter to Philip, on the fact that he does not desire to diminish or to interfere with Philip's powers, and he emphasizes the fact that he is dealing with a question of sin in which the Pope's jurisdiction could not be questioned. He makes a very brief reference to the horrors of war (religiosorum locorum excidium, et stragem . . . populi christiani), but the special feature of the letter, included in the Decretals, is the stress laid on John's complaint that he had been sinned against.

Innocent asserted his right to intervene in quarrels between secular rulers before and after his contest with Philip, but he did not endeavour to justify his action as based on a complaint by one of the parties. We shall cite a few cases.

In 1199 there was a dispute regarding Borgo San Donino between Piacenza and Parma. Innocent wrote that "inasmuch as according to the apostle, love is the fulness of law, dissension makes men transgressors of the divine law," and he directed his representative to require Piacenza and Parma to come to terms, and if they failed to do so of their own accord, to compel them, if necessary by excommunication, to submit to the Pope's judgments. Here it will be observed that the mere fact of dissension is treated as a sin, and as giving the Pope ground for compelling submission to his judgment. In 1207 Innocent wrote the Florentines requiring them to

make peace on reasonable terms with the Siennese, as the quarrel was the cause of "grave rerum dispendium," grave injury to men's bodies, and "immane" danger to their souls, while it belonged specially to the Pope, as vicar of Christ, to restore peace. He had accordingly instructed one of his cardinals to take the necessary action, and should either party prove contumacious, he was to deal with it by ecclesiastical censure.

In 1209, in a letter to the consuls and citizens of Genoa, Innocent dwells on the danger to souls, the injury to property, and the "personarum dispendium" caused by the quarrel between Genoa and Pisa, and on his duty to deal with those disregarding his orders. He refers also in his letter to the way in which the quarrel hindered relief being given to the Holy Land.

The last letter we shall refer to, in this connection, is one addressed by Innocent to John in April, 1214, a few months before the battle of Bouvines. In it Innocent directed John, on pain of ecclesiastical censure, to make a truce with Philip to last at least till after the General Council, summoned for 1215, was over, and it appears from the letter that he also wrote to Philip in similar terms. He gave these orders as the war between John and Philip prevented help being sent to the Holy Land and was causing other dangers, and he was therefore bound in virtue of his office to intervene. Besides ordering an immediate truce, Innocent directed that two arbitrators (mediatores pacis) be appointed to treat for a permanent peace. Should they fail, the two kings were to submit to Innocent's decision, and give guarantees that they would obey. There is no reference to any complaint by either party, and it is singular Innocent should have ventured to give peremptory orders after his previous rebuff by Philip. Possibly he counted on the political situation to compel the parties to yield.

The cases we have cited appear to show that Innocent held that as vicar of Christ he could require the rulers of States or cities at war with one another to cease hostilities and to submit to his judgment, even though neither party had appealed to him.

There was another class of cases in which Innocent frequently intervened—namely, where the interests of widows and minors were concerned. He describes himself as "debtor to widows and orphans"; and one of those whose wrongs he endeavoured to right was Berengaria, the widow of Richard I. In this capacity in 1204 he wrote John that he had given orders that unless he voluntarily did justice to Berengaria, he would be compelled to do so by ecclesiastical pressure. Next year he wrote again on the same subject, as the representative of Christ, who is no acceptor of persons and who does justice to all, and accordingly directed John to carry out his agreement regarding Berengaria's dowry. Should John fail to do so, an inquiry was to be made and the proceedings referred to the Pope for orders. In 1208 the dowry had still not been paid, and Innocent wrote to John that if he did not admit any obligation to her, he should refer to the Pope, who as the vicar of Christ was inspired by God in his judgments. John had failed to appear before the Pope, though Berengaria had been represented, and Innocent could no longer postpone action. Should he not appear within a month all lands included in Berengaria's dowry would be placed under interdict.

Shortly after his accession there was a remarkable case of papal intervention. Innocent gave as the ground of his action that by virtue of his office he was bound to give comfort to the afflicted, and he therefore ordered the release of Sibilla, widow of Tancred, and of others all imprisoned by the orders of Henry VI in Germany. It seems very unlikely that Innocent would have ventured to issue such orders except in the state of confusion in Germany due to the death of Henry VI and the dispute as to the succession. Innocent not only ordered the release of Sibilla and other prisoners, but directed the recipients of his letter to excommunicate those holding the prisoners in custody, and to place the whole diocese in which they were imprisoned under interdict. There is no suggestion in the letter that the Pope had acted as feudal overlord of Sicily. He based his action entirely on his duty as Pope to comfort those in trouble.

Crusaders were under the special protection of the Church. We need only refer to a few letters issued in the first year of Innocent's reign as Pope. In one letter to the Archbishop of Magdeburg and his suffragans, he directs that the property of all crusaders, from the time they take the cross, be taken under the protection of St. Peter and of himself, as well as of all archbishops and bishops. He also gave instructions regarding the action to be taken in the case of wrongs done to crusaders placed under the protection of the Church during their "peregrinatio." In the same year he gave orders to Philip of Swabia and to the Duke of Austria to return the ransom paid by Richard for his release while he was on his way back to England from Palestine.

An important function of the Pope at this time was to confirm agreements between secular rulers. For obvious reasons it was often of great advantage to both parties to have an agreement solemnly confirmed by the head of the Church and recorded in his registers. A case in point is his confirmation at the request of the King of France of an agreement between him and Count Baldwin of Flanders. It was, Innocent wrote, his duty in virtue of his apostolic office to provide for the peace and quiet of all, but it was specially incumbent on him in this case owing to his affection for the king and owing to the advantage (commodum) to the Church when Philip and his kingdom were at peace. He confirmed the agreement as reasonable, drawn up by religious and prudent persons, properly authenticated and sworn to, and accepted by both parties (ab utraque parte recepta). Frequently in confirming agreements the Pope laid down that any one infringing them should be dealt with by ecclesiastical censure (this would ordinarily be excommunication).

Besides confirming agreements, we find other cases in which Innocent directed the clergy to enforce orders given by a prince — e.g., he wrote the Archbishop of Guesen and his suffragans directing them to enforce the decision of the Duke of Silesia that Cracow should always be held by the eldest son of the reigning duke.

We have already referred to the Vercelli case, in which Innocent laid down that injured persons were entitled to appeal to the Pope for redress where there was no other competent court or temporal superior to do them justice. He quotes Alexius as urging this principle in an appeal to the Pope against his uncle, another Alexius, who had usurped the empire of the East. In this case political considerations, and possibly also the difficulty of enforcing an award, may have prevented his taking action. A remarkable instance of intervention, going apparently far beyond the Vercelli case, occurred in 1205, when he directed the Archbishop of Armagh to deal with a complaint brought by one Norman noble in Ireland against another. The complainant alleged that he had been compelled by force to give up his property in Ireland and leave the country and abandon all his claims there. Innocent's orders to the archbishop were to inquire, and should he find that war had been levied unjustly on the complainant, the aggressor must restore the property taken and release him from his oath. Should he disobey the archbishop's orders, he was to be excommunicated, his lands placed under interdict, and the complainant released from his oath.

Among the most noteworthy incidents of the pontificate of Innocent III is the Albigensian Crusade. The two great headquarters of Manichean forms of heresy, at the end of the twelfth century, were Southern France and Northern Italy, and specially the former. These forms of heresy had long engaged the attention of the ecclesiastical and of the secular authorities. As far back as 1022 a number of heretics had been condemned at a synod held at Orleans, and the matter had repeatedly come before other provincial synods, some of them presided over by popes. In 1179 the Lateran Council referred in one of its decrees to the open profession of heretical doctrines in Gascony and in parts of the county of Toulouse. The faithful were bidden protect the Christian population against the heretics. The property of heretics was to be confiscated, and it was declared that their rulers might lawfully enslave them. Those who took up arms against them were to receive some remission of the penalties of their sins, and they were to have from the Church the same protection as was given to crusaders. Two years later Lucius III at Verona, supported by Frederick I, anathematised the Cathari and other heretics, and on the advice of his bishops at the suggestion of the emperor, he directed that inquiries should be made by the clergy in every parish where heresy was suspected. Counts, barons, "rectors," &c., were to swear, if required by the archbishop or bishop, to help the Church against heretics and their supporters. Those disregarding the order were to be punished by excommunication, and their lands to be placed under interdict. Cities resisting the order were to be cut off from intercourse with other cities, and to be deprived of their bishoprics.

Innocent held it to be one of his most important duties to deal with heretics, as his office required of him to maintain the kingdom of God free from scandals. In April 1198 he despatched a monk named Rainer to visit the South of France, and he ordered the ecclesiastical and secular authorities to help him. He ordered them in the case of obstinate heretics, excommunicated by Rainer, to confiscate their property and to banish them. Should the heretics stay on after Rainer had issued an interdict, the nobles were, as became Christians, to deal still more severely with them. Rainer had received from the Pope full powers of excommunication and interdict, and the princes must not be displeased at such severity, as Innocent was determined to do all in his power to extirpate heresy. Any one who favoured or shielded such heretics was also to be excommunicated and was to receive the same punishment as those whom they favoured.

In the same year he confirmed orders issued by his legate in Lombardy forbidding the admission of heretics to any dignities; nor were they to be allowed to take part in elections. All podestas, consuls, and members of official bodies were to swear to maintain these orders. In the same letter he confirmed the authority given by the legate to the Archbishop of Milan to enforce these provisions by excommunicating any who might prove contumacious, and by placing their lands under an interdict. In a letter to the King of Hungary the Pope stated the penalties he enforced against heretics (in his own territories), and asked him to banish them and to confiscate their property.

Returning to Innocent's action with regard to heresy in France, we find that for several years he enedavoured to deal with the heretics of Toulouse and of the neighbouring districts through their rulers, but relations became more and more strained. In 1207, Raymond, the Count of Toulouse, was excommunicated by Peter of Castelnau, the papal legate, and Innocent wrote the count, endorsing his legate's action and threatening to take away lands held by him of the Church, and to summon the neighbouring princes to take away his other lands. A few months later, 15th January 1208, Peter was murdered. The Pope, acting on suspicion of his complicity, again excommunicated the count, and a crusade was started against the heretics. Innocent also authorized the seizure of his lands by any Catholic, subject to the rights of the overlord. The Pope had before this made several ineffectual attempts to get Philip, King of France, to take the matter up, but Philip was not prepared to run any risks with King John of England still on his hands, and he even attempted to limit strictly the number of crusaders from his

kingdom, but had to withdraw his orders in view of the popular enthusiasm. He also took exception to the Pope's orders regarding the count's lands.

After the conquest of Baziers by the crusaders, they bestowed it on Simon de Montfort, their leader. This grant was confirmed by Innocent, who also gave orders that each house should pay annually three denarii to the Holy See as a sign that Simon de Montfort would maintain them in devotion to the Holy See and to the true Church. When later on he was pressed to agree to the confiscation of all the lands of Raymond of Toulouse, he refused on the ground that he had not so far been convicted of heresy. Innocent, notwithstanding his treatment of the Count of Toulouse in 1208 in connection with the murder of the papal legate, yet had doubts in the matter, and was disinclined to press matters too far, but the more violent party in the Church prevailed, and at the Lateran Council of 1215 the lands already taken by the crusaders from heretics and those who had supported them, including those of Raymond, Count of Toulouse, were made over to Simon de Montfort "ut eam teneat ab ipsis a quibus de jure tenenda est," thus reserving the rights of the suzerain, the King of France. Raymond was deprived of his lands, as he had failed to deal with heretics and "ruptarios." A decree was also passed regarding heretics generally, providing for the confiscation of the property of any convicted of heresy or of failure to deal with heresy. The punishment in the case of contumacy, to be inflicted by the Pope, was the release of vassals from their obedience, and the lands of the rulers were to be open to occupation by Catholics who extirpated the heretics, subject always to the rights of the overlord. Provision was also made for annual inquiries by the bishops in any parish where heresy was suspected. The Lateran Council of 1215 thus ratified the action already taken in the Albigensian Crusade.

It will be observed that Raymond of Toulouse was not deposed for heresy, but for his failure to suppress heresy, and the suppression of heresy was declared a duty incumbent on rulers: neglect was punishable by the loss of their dominions. Heresy hunting was also now made a duty incumbent on the bishops of the Church.

The principles were those on which Innocent had acted throughout his pontificate, though he was much more inclined to mercy in giving effect to them than the more extreme, and possibly even than the majority of the clergy.

The exercise of direct temporal power by Innocent was confined to Italy. We shall deal hereafter with his demands based on imperial grants, and need only refer very briefly to his one material reference to Constantine's donation. This was in a sermon on St. Sylvester's Day, and we may assume, therefore, was primarily intended for an Italian audience. He told how the Pope, St. Sylvester, had cured Constantine from leprosy at the time of his baptism, and how thereafter Constantine had made over to the Roman See the city (Rome), the senate, his subjects, and the whole of the West, and had then retired to Byzantium and contented himself with the empire of the East. Sylvester, from reverence for the ecclesiastical crown, or rather from humility, would not accept the crown which Constantine had offered, but used instead of a royal diadem the circular orphery. It was in virtue of his pontifical authority that the Pope appointed patriarchs, primates, metropolitans, and other ecclesiastical dignitaries; while in virtue of his royal powers he appointed senators, prefects, judges, and notaries. In view of the interpretation by Innocent of the donation, it is singular that he should apparently never have made use of it in putting forward territorial claims.

Besides lands directly subject to the Pope's temporal power, there were many countries in which the Roman Church had at one time or another claimed feudal superiority for the Pope. Innocent was careful to claim any "census" to which he might hold the Pope to be entitled, but it was principally in the case of the Sicilian and English kingdoms (after the surrender by John) that he supported his action, as justified by his feudal superiority. In both cases it was of importance to the Church that no assistance should be given by the kingdoms concerned to a hostile emperor, and we can understand Innocent's enthusiastic acceptance of John's surrender, inspired by the Holy Spirit. Later on, after Bouvines, the Pope's position as overlord gave him a legal standing when he intervened between the king and his barons, and finally declared null and void the provisions of Magna Carta.

As we have seen, papal support had been forthcoming for John in 1202 when war was threatening between Philip and John, but it was now far more sustained and emphatic; and no doubt this was partly because John had become a vassal of the Roman See. Moreover, after John's surrender of his kingdom to the Pope, we find not only Innocent but also the barons and John urging this as a ground for papal intervention, and the feudal relationship was clearly treated by all parties as an important feature of the situation. Louis in his statement of his claims to the English Crown referred to it, but denied that John was Richard's lawful successor, and argued that in any case the surrender was contrary to his oath and made without the advice and consent of his barons.

Important, however, as the feudal relation may have been in the case of England, it was not on it that the Pope mainly relied. Even when he declared null and void the provisions of Magna Carta, he gave his orders as vicar of Christ, and the disregard by the barons of the papal rights is only one of several grounds for the orders he passed.

Innocent was not a man to throw away any weapon which might some time or other prove serviceable, but it was on his powers as vicar of Christ that his policy seems to have been based, and as we have seen, his claim to a right of intervention in case of disputes gave him ample opportunity for the exercise of those powers.

To Determine a Matter of Sin

C. H. McILWAIN

THE idea [that the Emperor had received the imperial crown as a gift of the Pope] was greatly strengthened and extended by the dramatic and forceful exercise of papal authority by Innocent III in the earlier part of the thirteenth century, the period of the Papacy's greatest actual power, though the Pope himself, as was usually the case, made his contribution through his vigorous enforcement of papal "rights," rather than by any new or more advanced theory of his own in support of them. Lack of space makes it impossible to set forth here in any detail his pronouncements. Over the Empire he asserted a power that was practically without limit, especially in the matters of election and coronation, but as his interference in these cases was in part based on historical matters such as the Donation of Constantine and the "translation of the Empire," they furnish less definite illustrations of his general ecclesiastical theory perhaps than his relations with France and England. It is noteworthy that even in England, which King John had surrendered to the Pope as feudal overlord, Innocent III's annulment of *Magna Carta* in 1215 was not based on feudal grounds. "It is upon his ecclesiastical rights that Innocent founded his action and upon them alone." It is probably in his famous decretal *Per venerabilem* of 1202, and in his claim of the right to dictate terms of peace to France and England, that the clearest indications of his general ecclesiastical theory are to be found. "It is not alone in the patrimony of the Church where we have full power in temporal things," he says, "but even in other territories, that we exercise a temporal jurisdiction incidentally (*casualiter*) and on investigation of certain cases (*certis causis inspectis*); not that we wish to prejudice another's right or to usurp a power not due us." "Three kinds of jurisdiction are to be distinguished," he says, in interpretation of the words in Deuteronomy, chapter seventeen, "first, *inter sanguinem et sanguinem*, and therefore called criminal and civil [*civile, i.e.* belonging primarily to secular jurisdiction]; lastly, *inter lepram et lepram*, and therefore known as criminal and ecclesiastical [*ecclesiasticum,* as distinguished from *civile*]; and intermediate, *inter causam et causam*, which belongs to either, ecclesiastical or civil; and when anything difficult or ambiguous arises in these [*i.e.* in things falling within the jurisdiction concurrently "civil" and "ecclesiastical"] recourse must be had to the judgment of the apostolic throne, and one who in his pride disdains to submit to its sentence, is ordered to die and to receive the plague of Israel, that is, by the sentence of excommunication to be separated from the communion of the faithful as one dead."

In demanding jurisdiction in the quarrel between the kings of England and France, Innocent protests that he intends no infringement or diminution of the jurisdiction or power of the King of France. "Why should we wish to usurp another's jurisdiction when we are not able to exhaust our own?" In this case it is not of the fief that the Pope proposes to pass judgment, but to determine a matter of sin (*decernere de*

From Charles H. McIlwain, *The Growth of Political Thought in the West* (New York: The Macmillan Company, 1932), pp. 231–33. Reprinted with permission of the publisher. Copyright 1932 by The Macmillan Company. Copyright 1960 by Charles H. McIlwain.

peccato) "and of this without doubt the judgment belongs to us and we can and ought to pass it on any one whomsoever." "For we depend on no human constitution but rather on divine law, for our power is not from man but from God, and there is no one of sound mind but knows that it pertains to our office to correct mortal sin of whatever sort and to inflict an ecclesiastical penalty on any Christian whomsoever if he refuses to submit to correction."

In one of his sermons, Innocent says the Church has conferred on him both a plenitude of power over spiritual things (*spiritualium plenitudinem*) and a *latitude* in temporal things (*latitudinem temporalium*).

From these and from other writings of his, it seems clear that the jurisdiction claimed by Innocent III was almost illimitable and his exercise of it without parallel either in extent or effectiveness. Yet it was a jurisdiction in its nature primarily spiritual, and temporal only incidentally (*casualiter*), a power grounded on the Pope's duty as Vicar of God to judge of the sins (*de peccato*) of all Christians, not on his right as a temporal ruler to administer law for his subjects. Innocent then in his official utterances appears to have made no explicit claim to a direct power in temporal matters, but it remains none the less true, as Dr. Carlyle has pointed out, that "it is in the Decretal letters of Innocent III that we must look for the ultimate sources of the extreme view of the papal authority in temporal matters which was developed in the second half of the thirteenth century."

THE PRIEST

The priestly aspect of the papal office is its most important function. The following selections aim to illustrate the manner in which Innocent carried out his priestly duties and the theory on which he based his conception of the spiritual power of his office. Augustin Fliche (1884–1951), Professor of Mediaeval History at the University of Montpellier and the Sorbonne, emphasizes Innocent's concern for reform of the Church. Michele Maccarrone (1910–   ), Professor of Ecclesiastical History at the Pontifical Lateran University, argues that Innocent had no desire to wield temporal power and that all statements seeming to indicate that he possessed such a desire should be interpreted in a spiritual sense.

The Advocate of Church Reform

AUGUSTIN FLICHE

WHEN we peruse the voluminous correspondence of Innocent III, we are struck by the multiplicity of bulls aimed at returning clergy and laity to the practice of the Christian virtues proper to their state. Calls for ecclesiastical celibacy, condemnation of simony, considered equally pernicious in all its forms, exhortations to bishops to lead purer lives and to be more zealous in the exercise of their offices, efforts to introduce a stricter observance of the rule in monasteries and to oblige married persons to respect conjugal discipline, such are the usual themes that appear one after another without interruption. In more than one aspect this apostolate recalls that of Gregory VII with a broader field of activity.

Innocent III first undertook the reform of the Roman curia. His biographer relates that one of his first acts was to purge its personnel by removing the young nobles whose scandalous rapacity and ability to make money from everything provoked the legitimate indignation of John of Salisbury. He likewise suppressed luxury in food and clothes, which had reached unprecedented proportions, and allowed it only on great feast days.

While demanding more simplicity in daily life, he also worked especially to promote the most scrupulous honesty. Some unfortunate customs had been introduced at the papal court. False bulls were manufactured in abundance to be sent to bishops in order to persuade them to pronounce sentences favorable to those who sought them by bribing a scribe. From the first months of his pontificate, Innocent sought to stop this practice which dishonored the Roman church; he threatened suspension and excommunication, he pursued those culpable, but he obtained, it seems, only modest results; for in 1204, as well as in 1212 and 1213, he was still complaining about the use of false privileges and false

From Augustin Fliche and V. Martin, *Histoire de l'Eglise depuis les Origines à nos Jours*, X (Paris: Bloud et Gay, 1950), 156–74; 180–1; 188–93. By permission of the publisher. Translated by the editor.

indulgences, which had their origin for the most part in the curia.

Venality was also repressed. Innocent III suggested as a principle that the officials of the curia ought not receive any payment, with the exception of the personnel of the chancery whose services were poorly rewarded. It is hard to say precisely whether these orders of the pope were carried out. The court of Rome continued to have a bad press, but we ought not to attach too much credit to the reports of malcontents who did not shrink at the worst calumnies. On the other hand, we must recognize that the orders of the pope were not always carried out and that more than one official of the papal court still tried to get rich at the expense of plaintiffs or those who came to ask for a canonical opinion.

The reform of the episcopate followed that of the curia. Innocent III attached great importance to it because it was the surest step towards a reform of clerical customs. As Vicar of Christ, persuaded that the religious life of Christianity was dependent on the intellectual and moral value of the bishops, he would use at all times the prerogatives conferred on him by Canon Law to limit the ravages of the spirit of the age among them and to compel them to practice more consistently the priestly virtues necessary for the accomplishment of their mission.

For this reason, it was necessary to look first to their recruitment. We have seen earlier that the pope had powerful levers at hand for this purpose. He could, while respecting the liberty of the electoral college represented by the chapters, examine whether the person of the elect met the conditions set down by Canon Law. Innocent III would not deny himself the use of this prerogative, but would use it with the sole purpose of preventing the accession to the episcopate of those who were not worthy. He methodically excluded candidates who did not fulfill the conditions of age and learning, while passing more easily over the question of birth: thus he recognized as Bishop of Worcester an arch-

deacon of York born outside of marriage, whose consecration the Archbishop of Canterbury had felt it necessary to put off for this reason, remarking that if the parents of the candidate were not married at the moment of his conception, they had regularized their union later and that he had a sufficient reason for a dispensation because of the learning of the candidate, the honesty of his morals, the purity of his life, the good reputation he enjoyed, and also because the chapter had chosen him unanimously, with the result that it would be unfortunate to deprive the church of such a pastor. The qualities of the candidate had, in this case, caused a relaxation of the rigors of the law. On the other hand, Innocent III had removed a too youthful candidate who lacked the knowledge to be a bishop from the archbishopric of Colocza, even though he desired to please the king of Hungary, who recommended him.

Before all, therefore, Innocent III took the position that the person of the bishop ought to be above suspicion. If he was, he showed himself ready to relax the force of the canons. He would permit a subdeacon to advance to the episcopate if he had practiced celibacy strictly as was required before passing over this clerical rank. But, when he was invited by the canons of Lucca to consecrate a candidate who had been denounced to him by others as having married a widow, as an adulterer, guilty of incest, a perjurer, and also culpable of violence toward deacons, he ordered a very searching inquiry and postponed the ceremony until he would have formed proof of the falseness of such serious accusations. Nevertheless, he did not hand down a sentence of annulment without having collected all the information that would permit him to avoid injustice: At Pampeluna, a bishop was chosen who was immediately accused of simony, extravagance, carnal weaknesses, and other faults against morality; the first inquest did not bring the desired certainty because of contradictions among witnesses; the pope ordered a second before ordering deposition or absolution. Likewise, he attached great importance to the attitude of the accused, whom he considered as suspect if he put obstacles in the way of the investigation and did not come forward to exculpate himself when he was summoned.

This respect for canonical regulation was marked also by a perpetual care not to infringe the rights of the legitimate electors. It was only when an agreement was impossible in the mind of the chapters that Innocent had recourse to arbiters, whom he most often selected from among the neighboring bishops, unless, as at Milan in 1212, he was asked by the opposing factions to designate the new bishop himself. One such case had an exceptional character. In general, when an election was annulled, the procedure undertaken followed canonical forms, and the arbiters intervened only if the division among the canons persisted. At Milan, before agreeing to the demand made on him, the pope had made many attempts to conciliate the opposing parties. At Fondi, in 1199, Innocent had annulled an election as much for defect of form as for the imperfection of the candidate; he asked the chapter to choose a capable and honest person; he was met with a refusal. Although he had the right, he wrote, to provide by himself for a vacant church in the impossibility of finding a pastor, he invited the canons to return to better sentiments; he even agreed to a short delay and threatened them with suspension from their office if they persisted in their abstention. It was hard to be conciliatory and respectful of the freedom of elections at the same time.

In summary, Innocent did not seek to enmesh himself in local affairs, nor to extend the powers of the Holy See to the detriment of diocesan autonomy. He desired only to surround episcopal elections with safeguards for morality indispensable to the good recruitment of bishops and the maintenance of discipline. Without doubt, he did annul some elections for a simple defect of form, *e.g.*, because the elect had assumed the administration of the diocese before having been consecrated. But was not the toleration of legal impediments, trivial as they could appear, creating precedents prejudicial to Christian order and to the regular march of ecclesiastical affairs? In similar cases elsewhere, Innocent did not prejudice the liberty of the electors in any way and, as we have seen, was content to allow the chapter to proceed with a new selection.

Innocent III above all distrusted candidates in whose favor the temporal power exercised too strong a pressure, and he combatted the activities of sovereigns with the most tenacious energy. Still, he gave proof of sincerely conciliatory tendencies. He admitted notably that every episcopal election should be undertaken with the *consensus* of the king and showed himself generally less intransigent than his subordinates. In 1211, he was apprised of a protest against an election which had taken place in Posnan, under the pretext that it had not been held in the right place, that the duke, a persecutor of the church, had been present, and that the canons had communicated with his chancellor, although he had been excommunicated by the Archbishop of Gniezno in full synod. The Canons responded that the election had been held in the Cathedral according to custom, that the duke had not exercised any pressure, and that the excommunication of the chancellor had not come to their knowledge. After an examination, Innocent ratified the election with the sole request that the Archbishop of Gniezno, who was favorable to the candidate, seek his agreement for the defense of ecclesiastical liberties which were somewhat threatened in Poland. We should not therefore tax him with intransigence or exclusiveness; but each time the threat was stated precisely, he sought to resist the rulers with an implacable energy.

This is not the place to dwell on his difference with the King of England, John Lackland, which has a much broader scope. It is enough to recall that it had its origin in the determination of the pope to prevent the invasion of episcopal sees by royal creatures and that, to forestall every attempt of this kind, to defend notably the See of Canterbury, Innocent did not shrink from using the interdict, which weighed heavily on the land for several years. The pope followed the same line of conduct everywhere. At Venice in 1209, he was not afraid to affront the doge in the matter of the election of the Archbishop of Durazzo, who, chosen by the canons, was refused entry to his archiepiscopal see by the representative of the government, then by the doge and his counsellors, who dared to pretend that no one could become Archbishop of Durazzo without their assent. The pope met the same treatment from the King of Denmark, who had tried to make the Bishop of Schleswig, Waldemar, archbishop of Bremen. Waldemar was an "apostate, a useless man, a rebel, and a defaulter," whom the king had previously imprisoned as one involved in a plot against him, but with whom he was now reconciled. Innocent refused this transfer, which was also desired by Philip of Swabia. Waldemar, however, took possession of the see. The pope, far from being intimidated, entrusted the affair to the Archbishop of Magdeburg, summoned the rebel prelate to Rome and, on July 4, 1209, asked Otto of Brunswick to chase him out of Bremen with his accomplices. Finally, everything was arranged: the chapter of Bremen, apprised by Rome, agreed and suggested the transfer of the Bishop of Osnabrück, which Innocent was happy to authorize.

In spite of all these precautions, some intruders were able to slip in at the head of dioceses. Although Innocent watched over the regularity of elections and removed candidates who did not present the canonical guaranties of age and knowledge, the proprietary wealth of the churches more than once tempted candidates who, without being positively disreputable, lacked the priestly spirit. Thus the pope, who had never compromised the needs of Christian morality, was forced to exercise over the western bishops a surveillance that the progress of heresy rendered more necessary still than at other times, since the luxury and negligence of certain prelates was in many ways eagerly exploited by the enemies of orthodoxy. We read in one of his first letters:

It is proper that the pope should be irreproachable and that he to whom the care of souls falls should shine like a torch in the eyes of all by reason of his learning in doctrine and his example. Thus, every time someone informs us that one of our brothers in the episcopate does not exude the perfume of pastoral modesty and ruins or tarnishes his good reputation in some way, we experience deep sorrow and trouble; in order to track down such faults minutely and to correct them with the requisite severity, we force ourselves to apply the remedy of apostolic solicitude.

This bull, addressed to the Bishop of Liège at the beginning of the pontificate with respect to the Archbishop of Trèves, who was under serious suspicion, contains a whole program to which Innocent III remained strictly faithful. In order to have permanent contact with the bishops, to know them better, to counsel them, to get them back to poverty, he ordered them to make an *ad limina* visit every four years, or in case of impossibility, to delegate a representative to render account of the state of the diocese. Without doubt, no echo of these interviews has come down to us, but it is relatively easy to reconstruct their tenor, for they were, by necessity, animated by the ideas which embellished the papal correspondence, where Innocent so often bared his priestly soul and tried to communicate the burning heat of his apostolic heart to his brothers in the episcopate. Above all, he recalled to them the obligation of pastoral visitation which, as he explained in a letter to the Archbishop of Sens dated February 15, 1204, made possible the reform of what needed reform, the creation of what needed to be created, and the provision, in conformity to the decree of the Lateran Council, for vacant benefices, and the granting of them to worthy individuals. He made the same recommendations to the Archbishop of Mainz, who, by travelling through his diocese, could acquit himself of the essential duty of his office: to nourish the flock entrusted to him by the words of Christ and the "bread of Holy Scripture." When scandals broke out in the diocese of Ratisbon, the pope ordered the bishop to visit the parishes regularly, to conduct personal inquiries, and to act zealously to remedy a disastrous situation.

It was the special duty of the pope to bring the bishops back to the exercise of their obligations if they had neglected them, and, in cases of necessity, to take sanctions against them. Innocent III acquitted himself of this mission with a paternal delicacy that did not exclude an energetic firmness. When disagreeable rumors reached his ears, he listened to them circumspectly; he informed himself about the individual who had been thus denounced, asked him to explain, and it was only if the accusations formulated took greater substance that he ordered an inquiry; this sometimes revealed slander. The pope was then the first to rejoice and was content to recommend to the prelate in the case that he should destroy suspicion and stigmatize the lies by redoubling his zeal in the exercise of his office. He did not want at any price to condemn an innocent man and took every precaution necessary so that would not happen. In 1202, a canon from Prague accused his bishop of fornication, drunkenness, also incriminating him of having sworn homage to the Duke of Bohemia, received the *regalia* from him, and delivered the wealth of the church to the counsellor of the duke. Summoned to Rome, the prelate excused himself on the grounds that the trip was hard, the time for consecrating the Holy Oil was near, and the son of the duke must soon be baptized. The pope declared him obstinate and suspended him, in the meanwhile agreeing to a new delay and ordering the Archbishop of Salzburg to look into the

affair. When the inquiry proved that the bishop was not culpable, Innocent was happy to forgive him.

Even in cases of serious faults, though Innocent never shrank from enforcing the sanctions he imposed, he proceeded with the same gentleness towards individuals. He sought, above all, to arouse recognition and manifestations of repentance, as happened in the case of the Bishop of Utrecht, who, accused of usury, confessed his sin to the Bishop of Sainte-Croix and received absolution, which he asked for with sincere contrition, in the meanwhile promising by oath not to commit this sin again. When the guilty showed themselves more hardened, the pope ordered a detailed hearing of witnesses to proceed, as was the case for the Archbishop of York, which furnished the reason for a searching investigation conducted by the Bishop of Ely under the direction of Innocent. The pope insisted that they hear the abbots, princes, and "other honest individuals" who accused him, that they likewise question everyone who was likely to furnish information, and that they transmit the dossier immediately to Rome for a decision. Also, at Vichy, at Bordeaux, at Besançon, the pontiff constantly demanded the results of inquiries being carried on with a careful respect for justice. At Bordeaux, the inquest conducted by the Archbishop of Bourges proved, after twenty months of testimony, that Archbishop Elias was "useless and unworthy." Innocent gave him two months to resign; if not, he would depose him and ask the chapter to elect a new pastor according to canonical regulation. And, as a matter of fact, Elias was replaced somewhat later by William of Geneva. At Poitier, the bishop did not respect the commands of the Holy See. He arranged to exclude poor clerics from the priesthood, despoiled others in favor of laymen, associated with excommunicated persons, and multiplied taxes. The pope ordered him to be investigated. He soon learned that these complaints were by no means exaggerated, that the prelate in question had allowed his men to whip one clergyman and to wound another seriously, that he expressed publicly his claim to be "pope in his own diocese"; he deposed him and excommunicated the clergy and laity who had supported him. We can cite other examples which give proof of the persevering effort of the pope to reform an episcopate which had for some time let itself be contaminated by the age and had given a foundation to the criticisms, in some cases justified, of the *Cathari* and the *Vaudois*.

In all circumstances Innocent was guided only by the higher interests of the church. Thus he did not limit himself to a demand for irreproachable conduct on the part of the bishop; he wanted him to be the same in his administration. There is nothing more characteristic in this regard than the bull of August 4, 1213, relative to the Bishop of Brixen, who was aged, ill, and had lost the power of speech. Innocent remarked that he was, on this account, unable to fulfill one of the most essential of his pastoral duties, that of preaching. His diocese could only suffer from this, and, he added, this ought not to happen, for the bishop was made for the church and not the church for the bishop. As a result, they should ask for the bishop's resignation and, in case he refused, should use force. His preoccupation with the same subject was expressed in a letter dated October 9, 1205, to the Archbishop of Mainz. This time it was a matter of the Bishop of Strasbourg's complaints that he had not been able to secure consecration in spite of his repeated requests. Innocent ordered this negligent metropolitan to proceed immediately with the ceremony, for, he said, the diocese had remained too long without a pastor, a state which was very prejudicial to it. At Trent, the bishop sought to retire because of his age, his sicknesses, and also his difficulties with his flock. The pope was disposed to accept this resignation, the more so because the prelate had sworn an oath to Philip of Swabia and had entrusted the administra-

tion of his church to the Patriarch of Aquila. But the bishop, with the agreement of his chapter, went back on his decision. Deeply concerned over the destitute condition of the diocese, Innocent entrusted the affair to the Bishop of Treviso with a commission for him to order the chapter to proceed to an election within eight days following the deposition of the bishop, and, if they refused, he himself was to make all decisions necessary to avoid an appeal to Rome — which would only prolong a situation already drawn out too long. In the interest of a church Innocent would go even to the point of sacrificing some of his prerogatives. In 1212, the Bishop of Cremona, legate of the Apostolic See, informed him that he had deposed the Bishop of Vicenza, who had not come when summoned by him and that he had ordered the canons to elect a successor. Innocent remarked to his representative that he had acted a bit hastily, that he ought to have referred the matter to the pope, to whom decisions of this kind were reserved; but, because of the "great peculation and the shameful inadequacy" of the accused, he ratified the *fait accompli* and ordered the canons to proceed to an election within the month.

In his correspondence with the bishops, Innocent stated several times his pressing desire to improve the moral level of the lower clergy. He asked prelates above all to combat the vices that stained priestly purity and pointed out to them the means to use in restoring priests to a more worthy life. In 1198, he pointed out to those directing the church of Jutland the abuses which had been introduced into this distant and almost inaccessible land. He commanded the dean who took the place of the bishop to call synods regularly and at the same time alerted Absalon, Archbishop of Lund, so that he might oversee the measures that had been taken. In England, the Bishop of Winchester received full powers to reform churches and monasteries which were dependent on him, to punish clergy who practiced usury and obtained shameful profits or who lived among those governing the land, with the recommendation that he should not show himself lukewarm in correcting them. In France, a series of very insistent bulls were sent to the dioceses of Sens and Auxerre where things left much to be desired and where the Archbishop of Bourges and the Abbot of Cluny were ordered to come to the aid of the bishops who seemed to show signs of some softness in repressing wrongs.

The reform sought by Innocent III brought above all a very strict application of the rule of celibacy, which he desired to restore in its integrity, especially where it had not been practiced. This was the case in the diocese of Norwich, where the pope ordered that married clergy should be deprived of their benefices; in Poland, where he ordered the Archbishop of Gniezno to remove them from ecclesiastical office and to suppress their revenues; in Denmark, also, he saw to their suspension and deprived them of their benefices, while interesting himself, with a scruple that did not lack delicacy, in the lot of concubines, who ought to be taken back by their fathers, brothers, or other relations. Several times also he referred to the legislation that excluded the sons of priests from Holy Orders, save in exceptional cases reserved to his examination. He also attacked all forms of laxness: he forbade long hair styles and lay dress, condemned without pity the worldly way of life and participation in secular affairs which could result in illicit profits under pain of loss of benefices or income and of suspension of clerical immunity. At Paris, a priest who was found guilty of faults should be put in prison by the bishop to do penance "by eating the bread of sorrow and drinking the water of misery."

Innocent III was not content to struggle against an undisciplined way of life. Conscious of the evil of the age, he pursued the wealth of the clergy which was often the cause of the worst evils. At the Lateran he obtained some results, but it was necessary that this progress should extend to all dioceses. Above all, it was important to put an end to the accumulation of benefices, the origin of all scandals. In a letter to the Bishop of Hereford dated March 28, 1213, the pope attempted to demonstrate that it was a crime against Christian morality:

The patrimony of Christ ought to be divided equitably among those who have been admitted to his heritage and it is not proper that, while some are drunk with wealth, others are hungry and fasting. Thus by the authority of the present document, we forbid you to tolerate it that those who are sufficiently provided for with benefices should obtain churches which are under your control by law of the diocese.

Innocent did not tolerate any longer that state of affairs whereby those ministering to parishes did not have the means to live. He learned that at Verdun and at Metz, in certain churches, "the patrons gorged themselves with ecclesiastical property while the clergy were forced to fast." He did not concede that he to whom the care of souls was entrusted "should not be able to support himself with the revenues assigned to him" and ordered the chapters of the two dioceses to put down these abuses. A similar reprimand was addressed to the Bishop of Ratisbon, who allowed clergy in charge of a ministry to replace themselves with vicars.

To put an end to these unhappy conditions, Innocent desired to enforce the residency requirement for priests. We read in one of his first bulls, addressed to Archbishop Walter of Rouen:

Since it is written: *that he who does not work does not eat* (II Thessalonians; iii, 10), we think it is improper and undignified that some clergy do not minister to the churches whose ample incomes provide for them.

This prescription was applied especially to the chapters. The canons of Troyes had received through the mediation of their bishop and metropolitan, the Archbishop of Sens, an invitation to annul an agreement whereby those who were not in residence would receive their entire incomes. Another bull, of June 6, 1198, reminded the Bishop of Angoulême that he had not taken account of the protests of certain canons about decisions made in their absence and, at the same time, a dignitary of the church of Besançon had been requested, no less imperiously, to stop avoiding an obligation considered essential. Besides, the chapters ought to give good example to the rest of the clergy in all things. The canons ought not only to subject themselves to the strictest exactitude in the divine service, but their lives should be above suspicion and by their simplicity should lend no basis for an accusation of luxury.

Such was the personal action of Innocent III to lead the clergy to greater purity, disinterestedness, and outward decency. He counted on the bishops to bring about the observance of these directives and put them on guard against the subtleties which sometimes seemed to frighten them. To one of them who was very well-disposed to put down concubinage among the clergy, but who, in the absence of any accusation according to canon law, did not dare to act vigorously, he declared flatly that, when the fault was public, there was no need of accusers or witnesses and that the scandal alone was enough to provide motive for a condemnation. To another he communicated his disposition to take action against simoniacs so that "purity and innocence would not be tarnished but the perverse simoniac would not escape the chastisement that was his due," and that because of the gravity of this fault, "in comparison with which all other crimes seem small," one could take the testimony of thieves, adulterers, and other guilty persons, while taking of course the necessary precautions. Concern about morality swept up this pope, often considered a jurist with narrow interests, more than any other problem. Scrupulous by nature, he desired only that "ecclesiastical censure should not oppress the innocent, but should correct the guilty." He wanted all precautions taken to render justice without misguiding them in questions purely formal, which risked delaying the sentence, and gave himself the duty of guiding bishops so that they would combine concern for equity with the benevolence of which a true pastor ought to give proof.

While personally exercising control with such vigilance, Innocent constantly made use of national and provincial councils, which were charged with engendering respect for the Roman legislation and adapting it to local needs. Thus, in 1200, Hubert, Archbishop of Canterbury, gathered at Westminster an important assemblage in full accord with Rome, which gave effect in England to the decisions made at the Lateran Council of 1179. Such was also the case at the Council of Dioclea of 1199, which reformed the Dalmatian church; at the councils of Avignon (1209) and Montpellier (1215), the one presided over by the legate Milo and by Hugh, Bishop of Riez, the other by Cardinal Peter of Benevento, where measures were taken to reform the church in the South of France and to prevent the spread of the Catharist heresy; and at the Council of Paris (1212 or 1213) which, under the direction of Robert of Courçon, proceeded to recast the laws concerning ecclesiastical discipline.

We find in the canons of these councils, among which one can find many points in common, the echo of papal interest. The Council of Paris desired above all to suppress venality among the clergy; it forbade them especially to exact a payment in money when they exercised the profession of law and had benefices sufficient for their maintenance, to fix a price for preaching, to traffic in masses and the sacraments, and to abandon their churches to become chaplains in another. The Council of Westminster did not authorize any payment for the administration of the sacraments and that of Montpellier ordered the bishops to give benefices to worthy clergy without charge. At Dioclea, simony was prohibited and the conferring of benefices by laymen was declared null.

The conduct of the clergy gave place to a still larger number of regulations. The Council of Dioclea introduced in Dalmatia and Serbia the legislation on ecclesiastical celibacy. Married priests and deacons were permitted to keep their churches if the union pre-dated their entry into orders and if their wives were vowed to chastity before the bishop. Besides violations of the law of celibacy, the dress of the clergy came in for some severe criticism. The Council of Westminster ordered them to wear black; that of Avignon, to have closed habits; that of Paris, to have nothing in their possession save what was proper; at Montpellier, precise rules were laid down proscribing bridles, gilded spurs, red or green habits, while making an obligation of the tonsure and of the hair cut in the shape of a crown. Distractions were also put under surveillance: at Paris, they forbade the clergy to have hunting dogs or falcons, abolished the feast of fools as well as dances in cemeteries and all sacred places. Canon seventeen of Avignon also forbade them in the churches and did not permit either races, cards, or love songs. We see in these various regulations the desire to avoid the possibility, as canon eighteen of the same council puts it, that the clergy should be an object of scandal and cut the figure of "the blind leading other blind."

Besides these interdictions, the councils reminded the clergy of their most positive duty concerning the cult and the sacraments. The canons of Westminster commanded them to avoid distractions during mass and to pronounce the words of the Canon distinctly, to keep the eucharist in a proper vessel, which they should cover with a fine linen cloth to bring communion to the sick. Baptism and penance were the cause for some curious remarks. The priest was not allowed to inflict on a married woman a penance that would arouse the suspicions of her spouse nor prescribe, under the guise of penance, the offering of a certain number of masses.

For Innocent, the reform of the church should not be limited to the clergy; the laity formed an integral part of the church. For, while the clergy were bound to celibacy, they had to observe the indissolubility of marriage. Innocent showed himself very intransigent on this subject. Marriage is a divine institution, he reminded the Bishop of Paris:

For man, made in the image of God, placed by a divine gift above the birds of the air and the fishes of the sea and all the other living beings that move on the land, does not return sterile to a sterile dust, woman was drawn from one of his sides while he slept and designated to help him; then this commandment echoed in his ears: *Increase and multiply and fill the earth* (Gen., i, 28). From this moment the descendants of Adam began to unite in a nuptial pact. The hand of the Creator, even after the Fall, interposed its authority to such a degree that, in the words of the Gospel: *Man may not separate what God has joined* (Matt., xix, 6). The sacrament of marriage cannot be considered as a human institution, because it appeared as an act of the divine authority. Thus, though it is contracted between human beings, it is in Christ that the bond is sealed, as we learn from these words of the apostle: *I tell you that it is a great sacrament in Christ and in the church* (Ephes., v, 32).

The divine law was, therefore, formal, and the pope was charged with insuring respect for it. If we attempt to disentangle the directives which emanated from the many juridical decisions delivered by Innocent III, we note above all that, in conformity with canon law as it was codified in the twelfth century, he attached an importance of the first order to the formulized consent of the espoused parties. At Modena, it was the custom, if the legitimate marriage had not been consummated and the spouse had afterwards had carnal relations with another woman, that the latter ought to be considered his wife and not she who had exchanged a promise registered in the church. The pope condemned this custom and enjoined respect for the Roman custom, according to which, "when mutual consent has been given in marriage between persons free to marry, this consent is enough, with the result that, if one of the persons thus united contracts another union later with someone else, the legal union cannot be annulled."

Practice conformed to theory. At Magdeburg, a young man married a young girl *per verba de praesenti,* then, without having relations with her, he gave her to one of his relatives. She did her best to resist, but was unable, in the final account, to escape the hateful restraint. However, she managed to free herself and asked the pope for authorization to return to her own home. Innocent thought that, according to strict law, she ought to abandon him who was guilty of adultery, but he felt some reluctance at allowing her to take her place with her husband, since she had had carnal relations with a relative of his. Nevertheless, he concluded that if she could not bring herself to practice chastity, it was necessary to force her husband to fulfill his conjugal duty toward her, for he could not blame her for an adultery that he had forced her to commit and should not allow her to suffer for a crime to which she had never consented.

Such a solution was in conformity with the law and morality of the time, which the pope always sought to bring into agreement, but it could happen that law and morality would be in conflict, in which case Innocent always gave priority to morality and made generous use of his power of dispensation. Although betrothments between children before they reached the age of puberty were null in law, he considered them as valid if the young people, when they arrived at puberty, remained faithful to the engagement they had made, and he did not hesitate to annul a sentence of separation pronounced by a bishop against a woman who, engaged before the marriageable age, had renewed her promise when she arrived at the matrimonial age. The dispensations that he granted usually had as their purpose the prevention of irregular unions and the facilitation of church marriages. He facilitated marriage between Moslems related in the second or third degree, thinking that it would be dangerous not to allow them to be consecrated by the church for, if the Moslem women had to fear the loss of their husbands, one could be sure that they would put every obstacle in the way to prevent them from being converted. As to heretics, he suggested in principle that the *Cathari,* when converted, ought to be allowed to remarry, because the former marriage was not valid, but they should not be permitted to do so in the case where one of the spouses had abandoned the true faith, for he had had the sacrament, which made dissolution impossible. He noted that this was the desirable way of handling the matter, for otherwise some would find it ingenious to pretend to become heretics in order to get a divorce.

There are other more banal dispensations inspired by the same desire to prevent sin and to favor regular marriages, while appeasing the demands of canon law. A citizen of Spoleto, while he was married, had kept a prostitute whom he married after the death of his legitimate wife. When Innocent was consulted, he put no obstacle in the way when it was shown that the husband and his new wife had no responsibility in the death of the first wife and that he had not exchanged any promises of marriage during her life. The same dispensation on similar grounds was granted to an Athenian woman, who, during the life of her husband, had known another man, whom she married on the death of her first husband. A knight of Alexander asked the annulment of the marriage of his daughter with a certain Opizon, alleging that at the time when the marriage was contracted, he had not known about the insanity of his future son-in-law. Innocent authorized the separation. On the other hand, he upheld the marriage of a woman from Messina with a man from Limoges — who had relations with her in the course of a trip and had a son by her while his legitimate wife was living — because she did not know her conjugal status, since the man from Limoges had died and the deed had been done.

He showed himself very generous when he was dealing with a country where Christianity had been implanted only shortly before. In Livonia, he asked the bishop not to show excessive rigor, while taking account of the youth of his church. He wrote to the Bishop of Tiberias that, if he had to regulate the case of polygamous pagans who were converted, he ought to vary the solutions slightly: all children could be considered legitimate, whoever their mother was, but the new converts could not keep their harem, because polygamy, once tolerated among the people of God, had been definitely condemned by the Gospel.

He was very strict when concerned with questions about a monastic vocation. A certain Hugh Vital had married a young girl in church when he was an acolyte and had consummated the marriage, then, after an argument, had left her and married another. He returned to the clergy, entered Citeaux, and was ordained a priest; then he had second thoughts and wanted to return to his wife. The pope decided that he should remain in his abbey and that they should only ask the young girl to surrender all claims to his adultery in order to preserve celibacy. The same conclusion was reached for another woman whose husband had been killed on a crusade and who had remarried after she had pronounced a vow of chastity before the canons of St. Augustine. After having had four sons from this union, she was seized with remorse and asked the advice of the pope, who thought that, since the second marriage was imposed on her, she ought to fulfill her vow. In an opposite sense, an archdeacon made known at Rome that his father and mother had had to separate because they were related in the third degree, and that he had not known if they knew about this consanguinity when they were married. Innocent did not hesitate to grant him the benefit of this uncertainty in order that he

might keep his priesthood and his office.

Kings and temporal princes of every rank had, like simple mortals, to obey the law of the church. Innocent III never sacrificed the demands of Christian morality to political advantages which would have resulted for him from a conciliatory attitude in matrimonial affairs. This is one proof among many others that the reform of the church took first place with him over every other consideration. He never wanted to pronounce the annulment of the marriage of Philip Augustus with Ingeborg; while he remained deaf to the supplications and threats that the king of France squandered on him, he did not dream for a moment of paying the price of doctrinal weakness for an agreement which could have been very useful to him in certain circumstances. Several times, he drew the attention of this prince to the responsibilities that he incurred before God. He observed the same attitude with respect to Peter the Second of Aragon, a docile vassal and faithful servant of the Roman church, protector of Christianity in the face of Islam, which he had crushed in 1212 at the battle of Las Navas de Tolosa. He had married Marie, daughter of William VIII, Lord of Montpellier, who had earlier been married by her father to the Count of Comminges, who had rather quickly put her away. After the birth of a son, the future king Jaime I of Aragon, Peter desired also to divorce her. He put up two arguments: first, that the first husband of the queen was still living, and, second, that he had had relations with one of her relatives. Innocent ordered an immediate inquiry, which his legates, favorable to King Peter, caused to be prolonged. Meanwhile Marie of Montpellier succeeded in informing the pope that her marriage with the Count of Comminges had been concluded against the laws of the church, for the Count had bonds of relationship with her. In addition, at the time of their marriage, he had already married two women and neither of these unions was dissolved by the church, with the result that that contracted with her was null. These facts were verified, at least in what concerned the second wife of the Count. There was, therefore, no doubt; the marriage of Marie with Peter was legitimate and, at the risk of wounding a prince whose friend he was and who was liable to render still greater services to the church, Innocent refused to dissolve it. He wrote to the queen on January 19, 1213:

He who is our faithful witness in heaven, to whom every heart is open and no secret remains hidden, that in the marriage undertaken a long time since between you and our very dear son in Christ, Peter, King of Aragon, your husband, we have never departed from the right path and we have not deviated either to the right or to the left. We have acted, as our conscience is witness, as in all the cases brought for our examination, for, by His will, we take the place on earth of Him who, just and loving justice, judges without taking account of persons. Thus, although among other princes of this world we feel for this king, by reason of his deeds, a particular affection and we desire honors and personal advantages for him; nevertheless, from the fact that it is a question of justice, as we are not allowed to protect the poor and honor the visage of the powerful, we can not and we ought not, neither to him nor to any other, grant the lesser favor since it pertains to the sacrament of marriage, which, instituted by the Lord in Paradise before sin, looks not only to the perpetuation of the human race but represents the union of Christ with the holy church, that of God with the faithful soul, that of the Word with human nature, according to the testimony of the apostle, who in treating of marriage expresses himself in these terms: I say that it is a great Sacrament in Christ and in the Church. (Ephes., XV, 22).

Once more Innocent considered himself the prisoner of doctrine before whose demands the temporal interests of the church ought to bend, so imperious were they. From this it is obvious that the theologian took first place before the diplomat. The rulers of Castile and Bohemia received the same decision as Peter of Aragon and learned that the law of Christian marriage is the same for all.

All papal interventions are therefore centered around a dogmatic idea and a fixed desire to put an end to illicit unions. The care for the restoration of the notion of Christian marriage is reconciled elsewhere with the charitable feelings that one so often meets in the acts of Innocent III. This pope, so intransigent in the matter of indissolubility, was interested in the lot of prostitutes, whom he tried to lead to a better life. We read in a bull of April 29, 1198:

Among the works of charity that the authority of Holy Scripture proposes to us, there is one of real importance, which consists in correcting him who wanders on the road of error. Thus it is necessary to ask women who live voluptuously and permit anyone indifferently and without concern to have relations with them to contract a legitimate marriage in order to live chastely. With this thought, we decide by the authority of these presents that all who will rescue public women from brothels and marry them will be doing an act which will be useful for the remission of their sins.

Innocent also sanctioned the attempts of one of the most extraordinary apostles of his time, Fulk de Neuilly (+1202), who among other pious works had dedicated himself to the relief of prostitutes, whom he received in several convents, notably that of Saint Antoine, where the preachers inspired them to lead a better life.

Along with prostitution the other sore on the society of the late twelfth century was usury. Innocent also tried to heal it. The condemnations levied by the Lateran Council of 1179 were enforced and the work was completed by certain provincial councils. In 1209, the Council of Avignon ordered a sentence of excommunication against usurers to be published on Sundays and feast days, and the invocation of the penalties set forth by the Lateran Council, if, after three warnings, they did not make restitution. It also ordered the excommunication of those who did business with

Jews in their usurious practices, which was the surest way of incurring it. The Councils of Montepellier and Paris put the clergy especially on guard by forbidding them not only to practice usury but even to lend money at interest. These assemblies translated the ideas of the pope, who himself counseled that usurers should be prosecuted by attacking the most notorious first, for some well-chosen examples would cause the others to reflect and amend their lives. . . .

The increasing development of wealth and luxury, which had led Innocent to work for reform, had aroused before his accession the indignation of men who remained faithful to the ideal of renunciation that Christ had preached and to which the apostles had strictly conformed. This conception of a more evangelical life, which was the basis of the Catharist and Vaudois movements, was not the monopoly of heretics and revolutionaries. It had been taken up also at the end of the twelfth century by pious souls desirous of reacting against the return of pagan manners, without dreaming of denying dogma nor of leaving the church, which alone was able to lead them to the gate of salvation. . . .

[*At this point the author relates the story of the founding of the Order of Friars Minor by St. Francis of Assisi. He stresses St. Francis' connections with the Italian mystical tradition and especially with Peter Damian. He also raises the problems involved in setting up Francis' high ideal for his followers and the danger that an unlettered group of zealous men might easily slip into heresy in their preaching. With this as background, the author then treats of Francis' request to Innocent for papal recognition of his order.*]

Thus, in 1210, after a year of groping, St. Francis went back to Rome accompanied by some of his friars. The Bishop of Assisi, who was there, arranged an interview with Cardinal John of St. Paul for him, and he, conquered by "this man of the highest perfection," facilitated his ac-cess to Innocent III. St. Francis explained with his customary simplicity the characteristics of the rule, which were condensed in three verses of the Gospels: *If you wish to be perfect, go, sell your goods, give them to the poor and you will have treasure in heaven; then come and follow Me* (Matt., xix, 21). *Take nothing for the road, neither staff, nor baggage, nor bread, nor gold, nor two tunics* (Luke, ix, 3). *Let him who wishes to follow Me renounce himself, take up his cross each day, and follow Me* (Matt. xvi, 24). Innocent III could only approve this form of the apostolate. It corresponded to his intimate sentiments and was only a variant of what he had counseled some years earlier, at the time of his meeting with Didacus of Osma and St. Dominic. Nevertheless, one reservation was imposed: The disciples of St. Francis were for the most part laymen without great learning, living by modest labor or by begging; the wandering life they led was not very favorable to the acquisition of religious knowledge that preaching presupposed and to which one could be initiated only in the cloister. But how was it possible to build cloisters given the conception of a mendicant order proposed by St. Francis? Such an objection threatened to compromise the papal adherence. But in the course of a second interview with the pope, the impression produced by the friars was so favorable, the obedience manifested with regard to the Apostolic See so entire that Innocent granted Francis oral permission to preach with the authorization to transfer it to each friar individually, each time that he would judge it necessary, but only on subjects of morality.

The basis of the Franciscan order was laid, but only under a very vague form whose inconvenience soon manifested itself. In the course of the years that followed, as the result of the increasing numbers of the "friars minor," new problems posed themselves. Since the evangelical spirit could not suffice for everything, some friars desired, in view of the preaching, to remedy their ignorance by study. Then the need for a precise rule made itself felt, without which the community risked falling into anarchy. St. Francis did not learn about it, but at Rome they were more concerned. Nevertheless, it was only after the death of Innocent III that the Roman church established an elaborate organization for the order.

It is nonetheless true that at the moment when the Lateran Council opened, to accomplish the reform undertaken by Innocent, great changes were on the point of realization. The church, faced with the assaults of heresy, had discovered the means of salvation. Tainted by the two plagues of the century, money and ease, it was turned with St. Dominic and St. Francis resolutely into the roads of poverty and learning. It desired to instruct by word and example, to ward off ignorance and to impose the law of renunciation, which was at the basis of its morality. Nevertheless, whatever may be the importance of the roles played by the founders of the mendicant orders, we should not forget that Innocent III had conceived and partially realized the reform of the church before their intervention, that he had had the great merit to foresee clearly the part that could be drawn from the movement toward poverty and the new forms of the apostolate which had taken shape at Toulouse and at Assisi. One author has written that Saint Francis "saved the Church" and "delivered Europe from the nightmare of heresy." Without doubt, he contributed, but does not the merit also belong — and perhaps still more — to Pope Innocent III?

Innocent III Did Not Claim Temporal Power

MICHELE MACCARRONE

BESIDES the phrases which are found in the letter under discussion, there are other expressions, characteristic of [Innocent], cited by those who assert that his ideas were hierocratic. Thus Arquillière hesitates over the words that turn up so often in Innocent's letters: "We who have been made princes over the whole land" and observes that with these words, Innocent "was thought to be vested with the government of the world." The phrase, as is immediately evident, is nothing else but one of the Biblical citations (Ps. 44:17) so often favored by Innocent and is frequently used in the Liturgy of the feast of SS. Peter and Paul (as well as in the Common of the Apostles, of which the office of the two saints is an extension), where it is repeated continually in the antiphons, verses, nocturnes, and minor hours, with an easy and natural arrangement. The later application to the bishops and, above all, to the pope became more common because of their succession to the apostles and was derived also from the first part of the verse of the psalm; the sons who have replaced the father as the mystical spouse of Christ are the bishops, successors of the apostles. Innocent himself, even before he became pope, spoke of this common interpretation of the phrase in the "De quadripartita specie nuptiarum" (Concerning the fourfold species of marriage), a small work which is nothing but a commentary, rich in allegory, on Psalm forty-four. In his discussion of the words in question, he observes how the fathers of the church had once been the prophets, whom the apostles succeeded as sons: "in

their place," he added, "bishops are created every day, set up by the church as princes over the whole earth." As for the particular application of the Biblical verse to the pope, it was suggested to Innocent by important precedents besides that of the Liturgy, especially by Nicholas I, who applied the words of the psalm to himself in two important documents: "By the grace of God, we have been set up in His house as princes over the whole earth," he wrote to the Archbishop of Bourges. He recalled to the emperor of the East that he had been "put as prince over the whole earth, that is to say, over the entire Church, because the earth is called the Church." The explanation which Nicholas himself gave of his citation makes it evident that he intended it in a spiritual sense, not referring to earthly dominion. The significance of the phrase in Innocent's writings is not different: he used it immediately in the first letter in which he announced his election as pope, and the verse appears natural and fitting to indicate the succession of the young Lothar to the old Celestine, as son to father. It is found thereafter in numerous other letters. It always has the same meaning as the Biblical citation. Never does it assume a hierocratic significance. We ought also to repeat that this expression is only one indication of Innocent's dependence on Biblical and liturgical texts in his style.

Alongside the words of Psalm forty-four, we can put another Biblical citation, usually invoked as an expression of Innocent's pretense to temporal dominion over the world. This is the verse of Jeremiah which

From Michele Maccarrone, *Chiesa e Stato nella Dottrina di Innocenzo III* (Rome: Lateranum, 1940), pp. 26–31; 37–42. Reprinted by permission of the publisher. Translated by the editor.

is devoted to his vocation of prophet: "Behold, I have placed you over nations and kingdoms, that you may tear out and destroy, that you may build and plant (Jer. 1:10)." The nations and the kingdoms indicated in the text express the universal mission of the prophet, not to the Hebrew people alone, and to the fullness of his power. In the liturgy, the phrase is applied to St. John the Baptist — he too was called by God like Jeremiah, even from the womb of his mother — and it is uniquely placed to underline the sublimity of the mission of the last prophet.

Arquillière wonders that Innocent applied this Biblical expression to his mission as pope: "in other times," he says, "Nicholas I had applied this famous passage to Michael, the Eastern Emperor; Innocent has taken the place of the emperor." Nevertheless, we must observe that, while it is true that the phrase had already been applied to the emperor by Nicholas I, Arquillière has forgotten that it had already been applied to the pope in the same century by John VIII, in a letter to the Eastern Emperor. In this letter, the pope claims for himself, with the words of Jeremiah, the right to correct and to reform kingdoms and peoples. Elsewhere, it was applied to the pope in a time nearer that of Innocent by Gerhoh of Reichenberg and St. Bernard, precedents particularly meaningful for Innocent III. The verse in question was therefore commonly used to designate the mission of the priesthood, and with such a significance was found in Gregory VII, who applied the words of the prophet to the legate whom he sent to Corsica to reform ecclesiastical discipline, and in Peter Comestor, the Paris master somewhat earlier than Innocent, who explained the duty of the priest to admonish by the words of Jeremiah.

In his frequent citations of this passage, Innocent III continued such traditional applications. Dependent above all on St. Bernard, he used the strong words of the ancient prophet to vindicate his priestly rights in the Church: as was the case in the letter to the king of Dalmatia in which he recommended his legates sent to improve ecclesiastical discipline, and the citation had the same disciplinary significance in other letters. At other places in his letters, however, Innocent saw above all in this verse the vocation given by God Himself to the prophet and chose it as a parallel to that from St. Matthew which was devoted to the calling of St. Peter to the primacy by Jesus Christ. We find such characteristic correspondence in the "Responsio"; it demonstrates the fidelity of Innocent to the homiletic canons of his time. The parallel was suggested by the fact that, unlike the other prophets, Jeremiah was a priest. Still, Innocent did not go beyond the parallel. While Innocent IV, who often used the parallel of the two Biblical passages, gave a precise hierocratic sense to the phrase of Jeremiah; this sense was supported by a favorable medieval tradition (originated by Clement of Alexandria) which held that Jeremiah was not only a priest but the high priest, because he was the son of Elias, falsely identified with the high priest who recovered the Laws under Hosea.

With Innocent, on the other hand, the phrase preserved its traditional meaning, and even in the "Responsio" the mission of the pope, indicated by the citation from the prophet, was of a uniquely spiritual character. For the rest, we have another document of Innocent that demonstrates explicitly how he referred the words of Jeremiah to the spiritual field alone. In fact, in a letter to the citizens of Sesi, a territory ruled by the Holy See, he distinguishes the two jurisdictions of the pope clearly and applies the quotation from Jeremiah only to the spiritual one. In the Patrimony, he writes, "the spiritual jurisdiction of the Holy See is not limited by any boundary; beyond this limit, it holds power over nations and kingdoms (note the use of the verse from Jeremiah), yet even its temporal jurisdiction is extended to many." The interpretation of Innocent is therefore clearly a long way from that of Innocent IV. Even when he used the quotation in letters or sermons, he desired, by means of it, to indicate his pastoral charge which extended everywhere and comprised all men, even kings. From the affirmation of his power over kingdoms, we cannot, in fact, conclude that such power was by nature temporal. Already we have seen how the liturgy of primacy had made such terms of secular government familiar, while still referring in an un-doubted manner to the spiritual power of the pope ("God gave you all the kingdoms of the world" is a statement applied to St. Peter in a response already mentioned). In two of his sermons, Innocent himself spoke of the "kingdom" which the Church ruled, but the context shows clearly that the expression was suggested by the scrip-tural text commented on by the pope and that every idea of temporal dominion is far removed from it.

*   *   *

. . . [T]he pope is usually called Vicar of Christ, and this shows that for Inno-cent the two terms [Vicar of Christ and Vicar of God] are equivalent, nor can we find a preference for the second. On the contrary, we can note that the former, besides being the more frequently used, has already with Innocent the proper and ex-clusive meaning of pope, which it pre-serves even today. In fact, while the term Vicar of God always stands with a quota-tion from scripture . . . , the expression Vicar of Christ, while often having an equal relationship to a Biblical citation, is also found by itself, as a technical term to designate the pope.

Innocent therefore impressed on this phrase the significance that it preserves even today and which, as is seen in Ger-vase of Tilbury, was immediately accepted by contemporaries.

In addition, by giving an official ap-proval to these words which designate the pope, he pointed out for theological specu-lation a new problem, that is to say, whether the pope received all the powers which Christ had while on earth and is His vicar. This problem had an immediate influence on political ideas because, given the then common doctrine that the "reign" of Christ was not only spiritual, but also temporal, it followed that the pope, as Vicar of Christ, held by right not only the spiritual power but also the temporal. This, in fact, would be the conclusion of the canonists and theologians from the thir-teenth to the sixteenth century and from this theological doctrine they would draw stimulus and support for the hierocratic system which pushed the parallel between Christ and His vicar to its ultimate con-sequences; this is precisely the reason why Bellarmine and the theological proponents of the indirect power were so vitally op-posed to the doctrine of an earthly rule by Christ, from which the hierocratic con-cept which they were combatting seemed to derive by necessity.

The theological problem of Christ's earthly kingship has also been the subject of current research. There was an awaken-ing of interest after the appearance of the encyclical "Quas Primas" [issued by Pope Pius XI in 1925], which instituted the Feast of Christ the King, and has recently been studied in some articles, written on the occasion of the same encyclical. In general, they examined thoroughly the scriptural basis and the passages of St. Thomas which affirm the earthly rule of Christ. However, their discussion of the theological question is limited to the con-troversies of the sixteenth and seventeenth centuries, disregarding the polemics, in fact, and also not examining the theolo-gians of the twelfth and thirteenth cen-turies. Their evidence is abundant and en-tirely in agreement, in fact, and in light of them it is very clear that the doctrine of St. Thomas, maintaining in some passages of the "Summa Theologica" and the "De regimine principum" the position of Christ as an earthly king, follows the opinion cur-rent in his own time.

While not wishing to study such evidence, which would take us far afield, we observe that D'Ales is not quite correct in saying that, in the matter of Christ's rule on earth, "the evidence is open to discussion." In fact, the teaching has distant origins. From a very ancient hint in the so-called Testament of the Twelve Patriarchs, it is next found in St. Leo the Great and, above all, in Pope Gelasius, who founded his famous distinction of the two powers precisely on the doctrine of Christ as a true earthly king. "Jesus Christ," he said, "realized in himself the type of Melchisedech, king and priest, and like this ancient figure is invested with a regal earthly dignity, and not merely a spiritual one." The diffusion of this passage of Gelasius, of greatest importance for medieval political doctrine, provided the occasion for theologians and canonists to affirm the earthly rule of the Savior. Above all, among the latter we find the most frequent evidence, because the passage, literally reported in a letter of Nicholas I, was inserted by Gratian in his Decretals. Among the canonists of the twelfth century, the testimony of Huguccio of Ferrara seems to be the most interesting. Commenting on the famous extract from Gelasius, he states that Jesus Christ was indeed a temporal king and also furnishes, as an example of the exercise of this power, the chasing of the vendors from the temple and the incident of the famished crowd in the desert.

Innocent III also held the doctrine of his master and his contemporaries, and it is necessary to record his testimony, because the concept that Christ was a true king was among the most common in his writings. In general, it seems permanently linked with that of the priesthood of the Savior; and the dual dignity, royal and priestly, of Christ are expressed according to his taste by two Biblical citations: "King of kings and Lord of lords" and "priest forever according to the order of Melchisedech." The royal power is always attributed by Innocent to Jesus Christ. The statement that even the pope, like Christ, unites the royal dignity to the priestly does not appear in his writings.

A mistake of E. W. Meyer has given rise to the assertion that for Innocent "the pope is King of kings and Lord of lords," while his footnote says in Latin only that the pope is vicar of Him, who is king of kings, etc.

Moreover Fiebach is mistaken in his interpretation of a letter of the pope, because he thinks that the pope claims to be "Lord of lords," while Innocent gives this title instead to Christ and not to the pope.

The consequence that royal power belongs to the pope because he is vicar of Christ, who is also king, was one doctrinal development that still did not appear in Innocent. For this development, it was Innocent IV who carried it to its ultimate systematization, when he asserted that the vicar of Christ "naturally and potentially" was king, even though he did not exercise temporal power. But as the text which contains the words just cited demonstrates clearly, the Genoese pope and the other canonists of the thirteenth century add to this theory under the influence of other doctrinal elements (like the theory of the two swords) foreign to the political thinking of Innocent III, and under the inspiration of the great struggle which dominated that century. [The reference is to the controversy between the papacy and the Emperor Frederick II.] Innocent III remained aloof from this development. In his theological works, as well as in his letters, the idea of the royal dignity of the pope is not expressed.

Lord of the World

JOHANNES HALLER

Johannes Haller (1865–1947) was Professor of History at the University of Tübingen. A prolific scholar, his major interest was the mediaeval German empire and his chief work was *Das Papsttum*, from which the following selection was taken. Haller was highly critical of Innocent III; he questioned both his policies and his motives. In his view, Innocent attempted to dominate the politics of his age. His efforts met with less than complete success.

FROM the first days of his reign, Innocent III let the whole world know how he felt about [the power of the papacy]. In the sermon which he delivered at his consecration as bishop — he put off the celebration until February 22, the Feast of St. Peter's Chair, for good reason — he recalled the words of the Prophet: "I have put you above peoples and kingdoms to tear out and to destroy, to disperse and to reject, to build and to plant."

The conventional title of Vicar of Peter was not enough for him; proudly he called himself the Vicar of Jesus Christ, the representative of God on earth. For centuries no pope had attributed more to himself and to his office; we have to go back to Leo I to find a similar expression of self-confidence on the part of a new pope. The same tone resounded at all times through his statements; his own office, his own person were put in the foreground assiduously in a way that none of the popes to that time had done. Innocent took pleasure, so to speak, in the demonstration of his power. If, at the beginning of his reign, he conferred an important mission of ecclesiastical policy on a simple Cistercian without office and rank, he did not fail to point out that he could actually have found important personages for this work,

since "all the members of the church were obedient (to him) as head." More noteworthy, we must remark how, more often than necessary, he relied on the fullness of power, the *plenitudo potestatis*, which had been given to the Apostolic See by God, and how he liked to underline his orders and instructions with a strong statement "about the forgiveness of sins." The office that he administered was not merely human. God himself spoke through him; he held God's place on earth, standing between heaven and earth as "Vicar of Christ, Successor of Peter, Anointed of the Lord, God of the Pharaohs, less than God, but greater than man." His empire was the whole Church, he was the bishop of all Christians; the others were only his assistants, on whom he conferred the power to represent him without surrendering anything of the fullness of his power. But not the Church alone, the world was also subject to him, for "the Lord had given Peter not only the whole Church to rule, but also the whole world." Without fear he spoke of his "principate over the whole land" (*principatus super omnem terram*); whoever opposes it makes himself the enemy of God. "The individual princes and kings have their particular domains; Peter is above all, with regard to both

From Johannes Haller, *Das Papsttum*, 2nd edition, edited and enlarged (Esslingen: Port Verlag, 1962), III, 319–21; 338–57. By permission of the publisher. Translated by the editor.

the limits and size of his dominion, because he represents Him to whom the whole earth and its dominion, the earth and all that lives on it, belongs." The pope is Lord and Master of all things because his office commands him to show justice to sinners and to punish their sins. Thus he becomes, by reason of his spiritual power, judge over rulers and lord of the whole world, Bishop and emperor in a single person, and the one who wears the crown as well as the miter. "The King of kings and the Lord of lords" — as it was said especially on feast days — "Jesus Christ, High Priest forever according to the order of Melchisedech, had established royalty and priesthood in the Church in such a way that royalty was priestly and the priesthood was royal and, at the pinnacle of the whole, He put him whom he had designated as his representative so that — since all knees, in heaven, on earth, and under the earth, bend to him — all men may obey and follow him and there may be one flock and one shepherd."

Aside from its frequent repetition, only the proud tone of the language, which did not hesitate at extreme conclusions, putting, so to speak, a dot on the i, was new in these statements; the ideas themselves were old and well-known. We know them as the doctrine of the French church formed in the period following the Investiture struggle and since that time taught in the schools as existing truth. In Paris, Lothar of Segni had learned what Innocent III proclaimed in the full tones of his eloquence to a listening world. He said nothing new to his contemporaries; the content was well known to them for a long time; they heard in the terms, words, and citations used by the pope the voice of Bernard of Clairvaux, who had already said the same things, often with the same words, fifty years before. What Innocent presented was the knowledge of his time, and, therefore, he hardly ever was contradicted. What was new and surprising was the real logic and relentless determination with which this knowledge was now molded into a model for action. There was nothing like it since Gregory VII had struggled against the whole world and was defeated. The rule of Innocent was also one great struggle, but the ending was different. . . .

Whatever Innocent undertook in Italy and whatever his success in these matters, it was only possible because the throne of the German Emperor stood empty after the death of Henry VI [1197]. For more than two centuries the fate of the peninsula had been determined and influenced by Germany; now for a long time this influence ceased because Germany was involved in the struggle over the kingship that was to last long years.

At the death of Henry VI the problem of the succession had still not been solved. The emperor's heir, Frederick, who was hardly three years old, had been elected king in Germany but had not yet been crowned. The fact that the opportunity was lost to bring the child, who was in safe-keeping at Jesi in the Mark of Ancona, immediately to Germany and to give him indisputable possession of the kingship by crowning him at Aachen was the misfortune or mistake of the Hohenstaufen party, a result of their lack of leadership, since the royal house lacked a strong personality, and the most respected princes were absent on the Crusade at the time of the emperor's death. When Constance was allowed to take her son to Palermo to crown him King of Sicily, his cause in Germany was lost. To ask the Germans to recognize as their king a child who had grown up in a foreign country under strange leadership was too much. In this situation there was no other choice than to allow the youngest brother of the dead Emperor, Count Philip of Swabia, who at first acted as regent for his nephew, to secure election as king himself. After a little delay, the election was held at the beginning of March, 1198. But only a few of the princes, supporters of the Hohenstaufen, united behind this action; a second group, led by the Archbishop of Cologne, once an adversary of the Emperor, were already arranging another election, and it took place in Cologne on June 9. They elected Otto, the youngest son of Henry the Lion. As grandson of Henry II [of England] and nephew of Richard the Lionhearted, he had grown up in an Anglo-Norman castle, learned French, and was a stranger in Germany. Two years before, he had received from his uncle, whom he resembled, the County of Poitou with its dependency, the Duchy of Aquitaine. He owed his election to the influence of Richard, who intended thereby to secure German support against France. The French answer was not long in coming: on June 29, 1198, a treaty was concluded between Philip II and the afore-mentioned Hohenstaufen, which obliged them mutually to assist one another against the king of England, his nephew, and their supporters. The struggle for the Roman crown threatened to turn into an Anglo-French war.

Nothing could have been more welcome to Innocent III than the fact that the forces of Germany were occupied by the struggle for the crown. This gave him a free hand to carry out his plans in Italy. But certainly in the long run, he had to hope that there would be a generally recognized emperor. His theologico-political plan for the world demanded the presence at its summit of the highest earthly power. But he also needed an emperor for his next goals. If his Italian adventure, the expansion of the states of the Church at the cost of the Empire, was to be more than a one-sided aggrandizement; he had to obtain the recognition of the Empire, which only an emperor could give. Therefore, Innocent already had decided to put an end to the struggle for the throne with a victory for one of the contenders. One can guess whom he had in mind. If Philip II was forced by the treaty with England arranged by the papal legate in January, 1199, to dissolve his pact with the Hohenstaufen, while Richard the Lion-hearted kept his freedom to support his nephew, it is obvious that the

pope was hoping for Otto's victory. That he did not favor a Hohenstaufen as heir of Frederick I and Henry VI was understandable in itself; but he probably favored Otto because Richard, who supported his nephew warmly, had promised by solemn oath to return all those things earlier emperors had taken from the Roman Church.

The struggling parties did not show themselves in any hurry to secure the favor of the pope. Philip (of Swabia) took the first step by employing the Bishop of Sutri, whom Innocent had sent to negotiate freedom for the Sicilian prisoners, to open negotiations. The French king took his side and voiced the strongest protest against the election of Otto as a shame and damaging to his own crown. He also offered to mediate an agreement on the old struggle over territory between church and empire in favor of the Church. Sometime in the spring, 1199, this message may have reached Rome. Somewhat later, if not at the same time, a numerous embassy from Otto appeared, with six members of the German clergy, led by the Abbot of Kornelimuenster, and with a chaplain of Richard of England and a citizen of Milan. They brought the certificate of Otto's election and asked for confirmation and permission to proceed with the coronation. Innocent did not answer Philip of Swabia and he heaped wrath on the Bishop of Sutri because he had lifted the sentence of Pope Celestine against Philip. That unhappy man, a German and a former confidant of Henry VI, felt deeply the change of times: he lost his bishopric and was locked up for life in a monastery.

The pope treated Otto's embassy differently. He decided to put an end to the struggle for the crown, and he thought that he was strong enough to determine the outcome in favor of Otto. He did this especially to make his conquests in Central Italy secure. He expected that Otto would not refuse recognition of the *fait accompli*. Otto needed the pope. He could not stand up against his enemies in Germany by himself, and the recent news of the death of King Richard of England put him in a position where he badly needed help. For well might he wonder whether John Lackland would aid his nephew in the same way as did his dead brother. This was all the more reason for Innocent to voice his support for Otto, who would probably be defeated and surely could not win without papal support. Innocent could also name his price. He demanded, above all, recognition of the states of the Church as they then existed and as he still hoped to make them, the Patrimony, Romagna, the Mark of Ancona, Spoleto, and the land of Countess Matilda, all of it with complete and unlimited sovereignty. In the future, only supplies for his journey for coronation would be granted to the emperor from these areas. Further, Otto had to protect the church in its possession of the Kingdom of Sicily, to recognize its legal jurisdiction in the city of Rome, to guide his relations with the Tuscan and Lombard leagues in accordance with the wishes of the pope, and to support him with money. He had to promise all of this now and to repeat it at his coronation as emperor.

This was neither more nor less than the abdication of the imperial dignity, which would disappear as an independent power in Italy and would sink to the level of a papal tool, if the conditions sought were obtained. In place of the emperor and through him, the pope would, in the future, control the political life of the peninsula. Still, the ambassadors of Otto agreed, took the oath the pope proposed for them in the name of their Lord, and put their seal on the document. On May 20, 1199, Innocent was able to tell Otto's electors that Otto could count on his support if he equalled and surpassed his predecessors in devotion to the Roman Church. He had already at the beginning of the month written to the German princes in their assembly, blaming them for not calling on his help earlier, since the question of the royal election, as he straightway explained, was principally and finally,

from its origin and purpose, his concern. He admonished them not to disturb the empire any longer with their bickering, and he let it be known that, if they could not come to an agreement, he would favor the one who deserved it. Thus, in case the parties could not agree, he reserved the decision to himself as the proper judge in the case.

In public Innocent could give the appearance of being an impartial judge because his dealings with the ambassadors of Otto were secret. Within himself he had come to a decision, though he avoided every binding promise toward Otto. For the confirmation, which the legates had promised on their master's behalf, was still not forthcoming. Time dragged on. Months passed without the arrival of any news. Obviously Otto was disgruntled with the demands of the pope, and rightly so. The young Welf had such a sense of his own dignity, despite his lack of knowledge of Germany, that the dishonoring of the crown demanded by the pope did not escape his notice. His German surroundings probably strengthened this idea in him. The excitement over the land-grab which the pope had perpetrated on the German crown could not have been a minor affair, for Innocent felt it necessary again and again to reject the charge that he wanted to destroy the empire as a pestilential lie and to point to his care for its preservation and growth. Otto and his supporters may also have been seized by the general mood; therefore their silence, which disturbed the pope.

While this stranger in the land hesitated to give his hand to the pope, there was widespread excitement among the princes of the Hohenstaufen party. After a long preparation, thirty-two spiritual and seventeen lay lords, behind whom, they said, stood many others, sent a letter to Innocent on May 29, 1199, in which they declared themselves determined to support Philip of Swabia as rightly elected to the imperial dignity as heir of Henry VI. They besought the pope in terse sentences not to snatch away the rights of the empire; they asked him to support Markward of Anweiler as Regent in Sicily and stated their firm intention of bringing their king to Rome for imperial coronation in the future. The apparent sharpness of the letter was underlined by its manner of delivery; instead of a princely embassy, a judge from Piacenza brought it. Philip, moreover, was satisfied to send a prior from Strasburg.

If anyone in the Hohenstaufen party thought it could carry on the policy of Henry VI without further ado and oppose the commands of the pope, he was very much mistaken about how matters stood and the character of the enemy. Innocent answered the letter of the princes with the usual assurances of his care for the empire, but he also let them know that he had to stand up for the rights of the Church. He rejected the demands they had raised and declared shortly that the coronation of the emperor would depend on him and that he would summon the one who fulfilled the prerequisites. He delivered a long academic discussion to the prior from Strasburg in the consistory on the superiority of the spiritual to the secular power; to this he added an historical review of earlier differences with election factions up to the present time and he raised again the challenge that the Apostolic See was asked for advice so late "even though the decision belonged to it from the origin and purpose of the office: from the origin because the pope had transferred the imperial dignity from East to West, from the purpose because he is the one who confers the crown." The written answer, which he delivered to him as a conclusion, Innocent later thought unnecessary to give him at all. The attempt of the Hohenstaufen party was without result, a drop on the water.

This occurred in the fall of 1199. After that date negotiations in Germany came to a stand-still and weapons alone spoke. An unequivocal victory for Otto would have seemed very good to Innocent; he de-

voted himself to that end in order to get English support for him and to keep the French out of the war on the side of the Hohenstaufen. In the beginning, he had thought he could obtain his goal with a command, but he had soon learned better. Philip II proved himself to be an enemy whom Innocent could not quickly overcome.

In the beginning it actually seemed that the pope had only to speak up. We know how the king did his will in the treaty with England; he promised to give up the alliance with the Hohenstaufen. Soon after this, a more significant sign of papal superiority appeared. A bishop-elect of Cambrai, a supporter of Otto IV, was made prisoner in the territory of the king and Philip refused to release him. But when the cardinal-legate who had negotiated the treaty, proclaimed an interdict in the kingdom, Philip gave in and freed the prisoner. Encouraged by these results, the legate decided to resolve the king's marital problems. And, since Philip stubbornly refused to reinstate Ingeborg, he assembled the French bishops at the beginning of December, 1199, and pronounced an interdict over the whole kingdom. He agreed only to a postponement till after Christmas and, in Vienne, on January 15, on his return homeward, he published the interdict.

The enforcement left much to be desired. The king had already appealed to the pope and punished those bishops who obeyed the order. There were only a few; most had agreed not to observe the command of the legate. Only when Innocent caused it to be proclaimed again by two bishops from Normandy and Poitou, *i.e.*, from the kingdom of John Lackland, did it seem to receive general observance. On this account Philip was forced to resume negotiations. And he met with surprising success. Innocent decided to reopen the case already decided by his predecessor and to investigate the validity of Philip's complaint. For this purpose, a new legate was sent no less a personage than Bishop

Octavian of Ostia, who enjoyed Innocent's special confidence. His instructions were very definite: to raise the interdict if the bishops who had been punished because of their obedience were restored, if Agnes, "the concubine," was banished from France, and if Ingeborg was restored to her position as queen. Should the king still ask for a divorce, the legate should hold court six months later on the question of the validity of the marriage, and the king of Denmark should be asked to send his representatives.

If we recognize that even the embassy itself was sent in disregard of the ruling set down by Celestine and meant a surrender of the position taken in the first place, the instruction was similar to Innocent's resolution: "to hold to truth and justice, if necessary, even to the point of bloodshed." However, the outcome was somewhat different. Cardinal Octavian, who met with the king at the beginning of September (1200), lifted the interdict as soon as the punished bishops were reinstated and compensated, and satisfied himself that Philip had given up Agnes and promised to reinstate Ingeborg in her rights as queen for six months. The result of these events was that Ingeborg was made prisoner in a royal castle. Octavian overlooked this and also the fact that Agnes, under the pretense that she was with child — she was only in the third or fourth month — remained in France. He set the day for court for March, 1201. He came to an understanding with the king which seriously violated his instructions. In his report he pointed out the danger that the church of France might throw off the obedience to Rome.

Innocent contented himself with pointing out in stern language the deviations of the legate and making him responsible for them. Whether he took the danger of a secession of the French church as seriously as Octavian is a question in itself. He had other reasons for not pressing Philip II too hard. Without the participation of the pope, Philip concluded a treaty with John Lackland in May, 1200, which, aside from serious territorial losses in Normandy, obliged the Englishman not to support his nephew Otto. This was such a setback to the papal plans that Innocent gave Octavian full power to absolve John of the oath to observe the conditions of the peace treaty. He still hoped to be able to bring English aid into the field for Otto. And if this did not succeed, he had to be concerned lest he drive the all too powerful Philip — who was already complaining of interference by the pope and his legates — into the Hohenstaufen camp.

Everything now depended on the court, which met in March, 1201, at Soissons. Bishops and nobles from France had arrived in great numbers; both parties appeared; the representative of the king of Denmark had also come. Octavian no longer was alone in the leadership; at his side was another cardinal, John Colonna, the one to whom Celestine had given the right to represent him, whom he had wanted to make his successor, a monk of stern, honorable mind. His refusal of the presents of the king caused a disturbance. The meeting began with the refusal of the Danes, on account of the relations of Octavian with the French king, to take part in the court on the grounds that it was prejudiced, and their departure for home. However, they were not disturbed by this occurrence and the trial continued for two weeks. It was expected that the king would lose the case. Then the clever Capetian surprised the world by withdrawing his request for a divorce and departing. He took Ingeborg with him, as though he was going to restore to her the position at his side that was her right, but actually to return her to her former position as a prisoner in a castle. The assembly, with nothing more to do, dissolved, and Colonna returned home in deep shame. What Innocent had warned his legates against as a hard compromise for the Apostolic See was exactly what happened: a proud beginning had met an ignominious end, and the words of the poet about the mountain that went into labor and brought forth a mouse had come to pass. But the sincere dissatisfaction, which the pope might have experienced at first, soon gave way to a keener judgment, when Agnes died in June of the same year (1201). Her death made it unnecessary for him to care for Ingeborg in the future other than platonically. His role as judge had ended when the king no longer sought a divorce; and what was the unhappy fate of the daughter of a king compared to the secular political situation which concerned the pope! In his efforts to win Philip II to his plans he was no longer hindered by the uncomfortable question of the marriage. Philip, on the other hand, had the daring to complain to the pope about the partisanship of the legate and combined with this a declaration of his willingness to undergo a further investigation if no other witnesses than his own were admitted. At the same time, he sought to have the children of Agnes made legitimate. Innocent did not hesitate before giving in, and he did not seek to continue the case. He declared the illegitimate children legitimate. Nothing more was said about Ingeborg.

In the meanwhile, Otto's situation had not improved. A few successes gained in the field by him did not change the fact that the Hohenstaufen party was the stronger in the empire. Until the summer of 1200, it seemed as if a favorable agreement of the princes on a third party, none other than Frederick of Sicily, would put an end to the dispute. Old Konrad of Wittelsbach, long-time Archbishop of Mainz and, at the same time, cardinal-bishop of Sabina, returned from the East but a short while before, stoutly asserted that the decision should be made on June 29, 1200. Otto must have been very much afraid of the result, because he called on the pope for help. Now, finally, the reply for which Innocent had waited a whole year came: he declared that he was ready to confirm everything that his ambassadors had promised in May, 1199, in his name. The danger passed, the day of decision never came. Konrad of Wittelsbach died and Otto met with a real success towards the end of the year: in a victory at Mainz he succeeded in capturing his enemy's treasure. With Otto's last letter, Innocent now had the bond in his hand which he needed to openly espouse the cause of his candidate, for whom he had until now worked only in secret. At the turn of the year, he made his decision and, on January 5, 1201, he announced it in the consistory.

As the judge holds in his hands the acts, grounds, and countergrounds in order to discover the judgment by weighing merits, so the pope, apparently impartial, spoke here, following only the facts and pure reason "in the Name of the Father, and of the Son, and of the Holy Spirit." First he pointed out his own competence in the manner known to us: the imperial dignity is subordinate to the Apostolic See according to its origin and purpose, because it was translated from Greece by the pope and for his protection and because the emperor receives the final anointing of his coronation from the pope. Henry VI had recognized this fact with praise by asking Celestine, after the imperial coronation, for investiture with the imperial dignity in the form of a golden orb. Since there are only three aspirants: Frederick, Philip, and Otto, it is proper to make a selection from three viewpoints: what is permitted, what is fitting, and what is expedient? Thereafter, the three aforementioned persons were tested one after the other by every ingenious argument of scholastic dialectic. By these tests, Frederick was rejected first. He had no claim, his election was invalid; his recognition was unallowable and inexpedient. It went worse with Philip. More than all the others, his rule would be a danger for the Empire and the Church, because in this way the inheritance of the crown would become a custom, and it was to be feared that he would follow in the footsteps of his predecessors, who, since Henry V, had been persecutors of the Church. Otto, on the other hand, was properly elected — for it is not the number of the electors but their intention that counts — fitted by personality and descent, and he is therefore to be accepted as king and called to the imperial crown.

We can spare ourselves the effort of following the words of the pope in detail — they fill seven columns in small print — we know, however, that they do not express his true motives. What Innocent presented was in fact only a mask and the whole artful, scholastic structure of his proof was no more than jugglery. Never have terms of law been misused in a more reckless manner to cover mere cold selfishness. Innocent did not make his decision according to justice but according to the advantage of the Roman Church. His real reason for supporting Otto was his promise to recognize the conquests of the pope. Certainly the world was not to know; it must believe that the pope had made an impartial decision on the basis of justice and truth.

The verdict was made; now it must be carried out. For this purpose, the Cardinal-Bishop Guido of Palestrina, French-born, was sent to Germany as legate. He was to go by way of France and the Legate Octavian of Ostia was to follow him, if circumstances permitted. It was his duty to collect the German princes and to persuade them either to unite in recognizing Otto or to leave the decision to the pope. In this sense, the coming of the legate was announced and ordered. Innocent obviously believed that he only needed to take a firm hand for Germany to obey his will. But then new information must have arrived to let him know that he could not count on voluntary obedience. He sent the legate new instructions and ordered him not to reach any agreement with the princes to discuss the support of Otto.

His foresight proved well founded. When the Bishop of Palestrina approached his destination — Ostia had to remain in France — disturbing news reached him. Otto had not been able to preserve his acquired successes. There was a decline among his supporters, his party was disbanding, and some already spoke about setting up another king. Only fast action by the pope, it was said, could rescue the situation. Otto himself later confessed that his cause would have "become dust and ashes," had not the pope stretched forth his hand with the authority of the blessed Peter. However, the cardinal hastened on his journey, and in fact, what he found on the Lower Rhine was rather discouraging. The pope's letter had brought on the worst consequences. That he or his legate should dare to summon the princes to an imperial meeting was too much. Only a handful of Otto's closest supporters accepted the invitation. In many places, the messengers stood before closed doors; in others they were hanged. Otto's cause appeared lost if the pope hesitated any longer. However, the cardinal brought out the letters he carried in which Innocent expressed his support of Otto "in our own and blessed Peter's name"; he called Otto the rightful king, ordered everyone to obey him, and excommunicated all of his enemies. This was at Cologne on July 3, 1201. Three weeks earlier, on June 8, Otto ordered a new document to be drawn up in which he promised under a golden seal to do everything that had been promised in his name in Rome before the end of the year — everything and still something more: he also obliged himself to follow the lead of the pope in his relations with France. Innocent had added this condition at the last moment in the hope thereby of overcoming the opposition of Philip II to Otto's ascent to the imperial throne. Otto resisted this to the last to no avail and, if we are not mistaken, he even attempted a little clever trickery in the drawing up of the document — it did not help him at all. If he wanted to be king and emperor, he must sign whatever the pope asked. He signed, but with the intention of not keeping the forced promises. And he remained true to this intention.

The impression of the Cologne declaration was strong, but not favorable. This interference by a pope in the electoral rights of the princes caused disgust in many circles. The word given out from Philip's side — that the freedom of the princes would perish if no one could be emperor save by the will of the pope — was not without success. Innocent saw that he had to point out again that he would not think of interfering in the princely electoral rights. He ordered the legate, Guido of Palestrina, who remained in Germany to promote Otto's cause, to proclaim his assurances on every occasion by word of mouth and in writing. Even the most noble of Otto's electors, Archbishop Adolph of Cologne, became hesitant and there was fear that he would forsake the cause. This proud Count of Altena, who once had hindered the plans of Henry VI, seems also to have felt that the pope's measures were an attack on his position. Innocent talked to him cajolingly, sought to calm his concerns, and to represent his own actions as harmless: he had only shown favor to a rightful aspirant. It served no purpose; for more than a year the archbishop remained undecided until the legate succeeded in winning him over by using his own subjects. It can not be proved that he won even a single vote of support by the word of the pope. On the contrary, a second meeting of princes, which the legate summoned, was no better attended than the first in Cologne, and the punishments he proclaimed terrified no one. The Hohenstaufen rose to their defense. It looked like a rising of the princes of the empire when thirty of them, about half spiritual and half lay, protested in a wild appeal to the pope against this unparalleled intervention, which contravened all right order. It had never been heard of that a legate had participated at the proclaiming of a king either as elector or as judge. The election was the affair of the princes, and if this was ambiguous,

there would be no judge, and the princes would have to come to an agreement among themselves. Besides, the legate would have violated the form if, as a judge, he rendered judgment in the absence of one of the parties. The princes demanded his punishment. This letter was carried to Rome in March, 1202, by a noble embassy, the Archbishop of Salzburg, the Abbot of Salem, and a Saxon margrave. But still we must note how unskilled the Hohenstaufen were. It was understandable that they should talk about the legate as long as there was no proof that the pope supported his action. But how could they misjudge the enemy if they hoped to have any effect on him? While the princes generally entered into the discussions, they had already lost, for in this area the pope was master.

What could they hope to achieve at all, if they entered a discussion after all that had happened? What was behind this mad protest but an attempt to come to an agreement? The embassy must have been strongly impressed by the pope during the negotiations, which brought no result, since he later, perhaps with some exaggeration, could congratulate himself that they had conceded that he had the right to approve the person he should crown. In general, they were somewhat less than strong in their opposition to the pope. They used the occasion, contrary to the bellicose tone of their appeal, to obtain favors for themselves. Innocent showed himself happy to do a favor; in the case itself, he dispatched the princes with a noteworthy answer. He presented his conception of the relationship between the empire and the papacy in a closed and well-rounded argument. He had not molested the electoral right of the princes, the less so because they received it from the Apostolic See. For, by it, the emperorship, in the person of Charlemagne, was translated from the Greeks to the Germans. Therefore, Innocent argued, the pope had the right to examine the candidate he was asked to raise to the imperial dignity. For, what if the princes should elect a despoiler of churches, an excommunicated person, a tyrant, fool, heretic, or heathen? Should the pope crown him? Not at all! Then Innocent turned to the complaints against the legate. His judgment in no way, as he was reproached, interfered in the election or verdict, but only confirmed it. There was no need for an investigation in the presence of the two parties, because Philip's deficiencies were obvious. "Since we can not under any circumstance alter our intention," we demand that Philip be cast aside, "the oath made to him disregarded, since such an oath should not be binding in favor of one who, as an outcast, is unfitted for the imperial dignity."

We know that Innocent did not invent the claim that it was the affair of the pope to examine a German royal election and to confirm or reject the results. We know that the kernel of the doctrine existed in ecclesiastical and French thought for almost a hundred years before: the translation of the empire from the Greeks to the Franks by the Apostolic See and for its protection, the conferring by the Church even of fiefs — this was often heard of. It did not go uncontradicted, but neither was it given up or disproved. Innocent drew only a logical conclusion when he saw the right of royal election as conferred on the princes by the Papal See, and another, no less logical conclusion, when he demanded that the pope give the crown only to him whom he found worthy of it. The conclusions might give surprise, but they were reasonable and the ideas from which they stemmed were old. What was new was the fact that a claim of an ecclesiastical school, which could have been accepted or rejected like any opinion, was proclaimed as a precept of public law. Whatever the church taught should be law for the Germanic-Roman empire. Certainly, this claim was no mere discovery; it developed from the doctrine that the spiritual power surpassed all worldly power and especially that the Roman Empire was dependent on the church. Innocent confirmed this reasoning

by a borrowing from the Canon Law: whoever consecrated should, as he held, examine the one who was to be consecrated. This was true also for the emperor, whom the pope must consecrate. In this sense, the answer of Innocent III to the protest of the German princes formed the conclusion of a church doctrine and its proclamation into a law which would allow no contradiction. Innocent placed the edict in a collection of decretals, which would serve the Church as a law book and, in later expanded versions, endured for centuries. We find, in the section dealing with elections, his edict on the authority of the pope in the imperial election, the decretal "Venerabilem," as it was called from the first word. Thereby, the election of the German king was made a part of canon law.

We might very well put the question whether this document — it takes for granted the general basis from which it arose — fulfilled its purpose, whether the judgment against Philip and in favor of Otto was well founded. The question whether the decretal deserves the reputation of precedent for further decisions as does the declaration of January 5, 1201 — repeated in part word for word — does not allow an affirmative answer. How small is the sharp distinction between judgment and confirmation, as if a confirmation in such a case contained no judgment! How wrong the pope was in his facts about the confirmation of the elections of Lothar and Konrad III, as if the situation of things then and his treatment of the declarations of Honorius II and Innocent II had the least similarity to the present! Unofficially, the accusation was made against Philip that he himself had taken the oath of loyalty to his nephew Frederick and therefore, as an oath-breaker, could not be king. Was it right to exclude Philip because of the deeds of his predecessors? According to the German view, inheritance of the crown by the same family was natural, and royal blood conferred a claim on it. This was violated when Innocent viewed the kingship of Philip as a threat to [his goal of] preventing hereditary monarchy. Likewise, the statement that Philip was not eligible for election because he was excommunicated was dishonest. Innocent, the cardinal of 1196, who had witnessed Celestine's decision, knew that it was directed in a general way against all who had attacked the Patrimony of Peter, without naming Philip. Innocent the lawyer knew that only excommunication by name could render election impossible. Finally, as for Otto, Innocent had earlier reckoned as his special virtue the fact that, in contrast to the Hohenstaufen, his ancestors had been loyal to the church. He did not repeat this now. And for good reason. Could one praise in any way Otto's maternal grandfather, Henry II of England, the inspirer of the murder of Thomas à Becket, for his special loyalty to the church? Also, the Germans knew only too well how Henry the Lion, Otto's father, had treated churches and clergy. Among the reasons for which the imperial court banished him, the mistreatment and despoiling of churches was preeminent. The pope was clever not to waste any words on Otto's personal fitness. On what did he therefore base his decision in favor of Otto? Merely on the fact of his elevation, the very fact on which few in the whole world were in agreement.

Innocent III did better work elsewhere; the decretal "Venerabilem" is no masterpiece. It is presented as the just judgment of a judge and reveals itself in every line as the partisan work of a pettifogging lawyer, a web spun out of willful distortions. It was viewed in this way by many contemporaries even then. The Swabian prior Burchard of Ursberg, a clever, learned, and worldly-wise man, recorded in his chronicle the stout-hearted judgment that the pope had not rendered a just decision and had stated many senseless and false things in his letters to the princes. The actual fact was that this ceremonial manifestation seemed to make no impression at all. Not one of the German princes changed sides after this; there was no weakening of the Hohenstaufen party. Not even the bishops

were concerned over the threat of ecclesiastical censure. Indeed, the pope did have many alternatives at hand in order to influence individuals: here was an individual whose life was not blameless, there one who had not obtained office properly; archbishops needed the pallium; others were engaged in court cases. But it is obvious how little the pope accomplished. When he invited one of the most guilty to Rome, he did not always know who would draw up the letters and had to have the legate fill in the addresses. The letters probably did not even arrive at their destination. In Mainz, where a double election had taken place, the Hohenstaufen party refused to accept the decision of the legate, accused him of taking a bribe, and complained about him to the pope. And when Innocent came to his legate's help, it was of no avail; the Hohenstaufen candidate prevailed. Where someone preferred to save himself difficulty by outward conformity, it was only for an advantage. Obligations accepted were not fulfilled; they were rejected or voided of application by conditions. Innocent himself seems to have felt that his actions were without success, for he showed a tendency to mete out softer punishments. There was no talk of direct action; rather it seemed that he was lacking in the necessary severity and determination. His threat to deprive the disobedient Archbishop of Trier of the dignity of a metropolitan came to nothing and, in other cases, he usually did nothing. He received a strong answer from the Bishop of Halberstadt, whom he tried personally to persuade to abandon Philip, to the effect that he would rather be accused of disobedience than of breaking an oath. Some had already pointed out that the pope quarreled with the cardinals who would not agree with his conduct. Innocent felt it necessary to deny this in a wordy, preachy letter and to permit the cardinals to witness this fact with a public declaration. But he must have seen that he could not continue on his chosen path, because at the end of the year he decided to bring a year of peace to the contending parties. He did this while under serious attack so that some had little confidence that he had only the welfare of the empire in mind. Indeed, he did not hesitate to confess in view of the spread of heresy "that the spiritual sword would often be useless if the secular sword did not assist it." His command, like all earlier ones, met with no success. His policy was not even successful in his own country: in Lombardy he could not secure support for his advice and actions and recognition of Otto as king.

In the meantime, his legate was more successful than the pope, but not in the use of spiritual weapons. Guido of Palestrina knew very well how to strengthen Otto's supporters by worldly advantages and to win new ones in the same way. He restored the broken unity of the princes of the Netherlands, Otto's strongest allies, secured the support of the Archbishop of Cologne by the fact that, among other things, he secured the abolition of burdensome taxes in the capital; he strengthened the alliance between Otto and the King of Denmark; thus he finally succeeded in drawing two of the mightiest princes from the Hohenstaufen to the Welf side. The Landgrave of Thuringia, who once went over to Philip for a high price, returned to Otto. The King of Bohemia agreed to desert Philip for the recognition of his royal title and the advantages offered the bishopric of Prague. For that reason, the cardinal was not afraid of the difficult trip to Bohemia. The results of these switches of allegiance were soon evident. Until the beginning of the year 1203, the forces of the two parties were about equal; Otto was recognized in the Northwest, Philip in the East and South. In the summer of 1203, Otto gained a significant advantage. In the attempt to control Thuringia by force, Philip was bested and his retreat was the same as a rout. Even earlier he had viewed his situation with so little confidence that he attempted to come to an agreement with the pope. Innocent, driven from Rome by the urban unrest discussed earlier, and pressed by difficulties, agreed to secret negotiations of an unofficial sort. But they met no success, though Philip was not sparing with his promises elsewhere — freedom of episcopal elections, surrender of the inheritance of prelates, a law that would have tightened the control of the imperial ban by the pope, marriage of a daughter with a nephew of the pope, and the subordination of the church of Constantinople to the Apostolic See — because, in the points that were important to Innocent, he made no significant concessions. He would give back what had been taken improperly from the Roman church by himself or his predecessors. This was not enough for the pope; Otto had bound himself without ambiguity. Besides, the secret was not kept, and Innocent had to lie about his representatives.

Disregarding the latest success of Otto, there was still no end in sight to the struggle over the German crown, and it was too early to expect a decision by war. The decision came at another place, in the Anglo-French war, and it was against Otto and his protector, the pope.

Innocent III as Judge

BRIAN TIERNEY

The theoretical basis on which Innocent III founded his conception of the temporal power of the papacy forms one of the underlying themes of the readings in this book. Brian Tierney (b. 1922) attempts in the following selection to analyze the meaning of Innocent's decretal, *Per Venerabilem*, in order to show that Innocent did claim extensive temporal jurisdiction in legal matters. Professor Tierney was educated at Cambridge University and taught at the Catholic University of America prior to accepting the Professorship of Mediaeval History at Cornell University. His special interests lie in the field of mediaeval law and representative institutions.

I N 1202, Count William of Montpellier persuaded the archbishop of Arles to intercede with the pope concerning the legitimization of the count's bastard children. It was not that he wanted his boys to be eligible to become priests, the usual reason for a papal dispensation *ex defectu natalium;* the count was anxious that his children should enjoy all the rights of legitimate offspring in the temporal sphere as well. Pope Innocent III had recently granted this privilege to the children of King Philip II by Agnes de Meran, and Count William hoped to obtain a similar favor.

The pope refused this request. He had just reached an agreement with Philip about the king's matrimonial difficulties and no doubt did not wish to provoke him anew by an officious intervention in a case that evidently pertained to the royal jurisdiction. But Innocent III was not content to leave the matter at that. He wanted there to be no doubt that the pope did have extensive powers in secular affairs even though he was not choosing to exercise them in this particular case. Hence his reply to Count William was cast in the form of the famous decretal *Per Venerabilem;* in which Innocent took advantage of this relatively trivial occasion to inject into the mainstream of mediaeval canon law a series of far-reaching pronouncements concerning the juridical rights of the pope in secular disputes. The decretal was included first in the unofficial compilation of Alanus and then in the officially promulgated collection of canons known as the *Compilatio Tertia.* Innocent ensured that no jot or tittle of his carefully chosen terminology should pass into oblivion or lack adequate canonistic exegesis when he sent a copy of this compilation to the university of Bologna with instructions that henceforward it was to be used "both in trials and in the schools." The pope's phrases were indeed discussed eagerly in the schools by generations of mediaeval canonists; more recently their implications have been debated with almost equal vigor by modern historians.

The decretal was full of meat. Innocent's apparently innocuous, incidental comment that the king of France recognized no tem-

From Brian Tierney, " 'Tria Quippe Distinguit Iudicia . . .' A Note on Innocent III's Decretal *Per Venerabilem," Speculum,* XXXVII (1962), 48–59. By permission of the editors of *Speculum* and The Mediaeval Academy of America. Quotations which appeared in the original in Latin have been translated by the editor.

poral superior provided a canonical basis for a whole theory of the independence of national kingdoms from the empire, which in turn has given rise to an elaborate controversy among modern historians about the origins of national sovereignty in Europe. As for the immediate occasion of the letter, the pope held that authority to legitimize for spiritual functions necessarily included a capacity to legitimize in the temporal sphere as well "because for spiritualities greater care and authority and worthiness are required." This also gave rise to an important canonical controversy. But the greatest significance of the decretal for students of mediaeval political theory lies in the fact that, having made these points and having protested that he had no wish to usurp the jurisdiction of another, Innocent went on to give a more general explanation of the pope's right to intervene in secular affairs:

> Motivated, therefore, by these reasons, we did the favor asked for by the king, drawing justification from both the Old and New Testament, because we exercise temporal jurisdiction not only in the patrimony of the church (over which we have full power in temporal affairs), but also in other regions, in certain cases, we exercise this power incidentally.

The Old Testament proof was a passage from Deuteronomy (xvii. 8–12) "If thou perceive that there be among you a hard and doubtful matter in judgment between blood and blood, cause and cause, leprosy and leprosy; and thou see that the words of the judges within thy gates do vary: arise and go up to the place which the Lord thy God shall choose. And thou shalt come to the priests of the Levitical race and to the judge that shall be at that time . . . And thou shalt do whatsoever they shall say." The New Testament was cited (Matthew xvi. 19, "Whatsoever thou shalt bind on earth it shall be bound in heaven") to demonstrate that in the new dispensation the apostolic see was evidently the "chosen place" of God, and the pope

himself the judge who presided there. And so Innocent reached his conclusion:

> There are, to be sure, three distinct kinds of cases: First between blood and blood, for which reason it is called criminal and, also, civil. The last between leper and leper, for which reason it is known as ecclesiastical and, also, criminal. In the middle between case and case, which is referred to both, the ecclesiastical and the civil; when there is something difficult or ambiguous in these matters [*in quibus*], it must be referred to the Apostolic See: whoever in his pride refuses to observe this sentence is condemned to death, that is, to be separated from the communion of the faithful by the sentence of excommunication like one dead.

The interpretation of this passage is of crucial importance for the whole much-controverted question whether Pope Innocent III was essentially "dualistic" or "hierocratic" in his theory of the relations of church and state. It was already well established that in the strictly ecclesiastical sphere all "hard and doubtful matters," the so-called *causae arduae*, were to be referred to the apostolic see for decision. The question is whether Innocent was simply extending that claim to the sphere of secular jurisdiction or whether his words were intended to convey some other meaning. It happens that the two outstandingly superior textbooks on mediaeval political theory in current use offer distorted interpretations of the pope's words and that the distortion has not been discussed, nor the passage adequately analysed in any of the recent specialist works on Innocent's political theory. A note of correction therefore seems in order.

A. J. Carlyle saw in *Per Venerabilem* only a claim that "in cases of conflict between the spiritual and temporal jurisdiction, the spiritual power is to decide." C. H. McIlwain similarly supposed that the "third judgment" referred only to those matters that were "in the first instance concurrently within the jurisdiction of both temporal and spiritual courts." With his usual discernment, however, McIlwain added that this was not the only possible interpretation of the passage. "If the words 'in these' . . . refer back to all three kinds of jurisdiction, then the interpretation above is wrong, and Innocent IV later added practically nothing to the claim of his predecessor."

Innocent III's grouping of clauses does suggest that he intended the "in quibus" to refer particularly to the third type of judgment. But it seems quite certain that he did not intend to exclude the first two types of cases from papal jurisdiction, and there can be no reasonable doubt that, in the third class of cases, he intended to include all lawsuits, whether ecclesiastical or secular, and not merely those cases that had an ecclesiastical as well as a secular aspect.

As to the first point, one has only to consider the nature of the first two types of judgment. One of them was "ecclesiasticum et criminale." That is to say it had reference to criminal cases that fell within the jurisdiction of the spiritual courts, such as heresy or sacrilege. Obviously the pope was not intending to exclude himself from the role of judging such cases; the very essence of the papal position was to be supreme judge, *iudex ordinarius omnium*, at least in spiritualities. The other class of criminal cases mentioned, "inter sanguinem et sanguinem," was defined as "criminale . . . et civile." That is to say it referred to crimes like murder or assault normally cognizable before a secular judge. But Innocent could not have intended to exclude matters of this kind from the sphere of papal judgment for, in the decretal, *Novit* (1204), he explicitly claimed the right to intervene in such cases *ratione peccati* [on account of sin]. A crime of violence was also a sin, and all cases involving sin pertained to the papal jurisdiction according to Innocent.

The ambiguous definition of the third class of cases ("inter causam et causam quod ad utrumque refertur tam ecclesiasticum quam civile") offers greater difficulties of interpretation. The first argument

against the view of Carlyle and McIlwain that Innocent's words referred only to cases where the spiritual and temporal jurisdictions overlapped is an *argumentum ex silentio*. It did not occur to any contemporary canonist that the pope's phrases could possibly have the meaning attributed to them by the modern historians. The point is of some significance, for several of the early commentaries on the *Compilatio Tertia* were written by canonists who are known as convinced dualists, e.g., Laurentius Hispanus, Vincentius Hispanus, and Johannes Teutonicus. These men were all interested in defending the essential autonomy of the secular power against the hierocratic views of contemporaries like Alanus and Tancred who maintained that supreme spiritual and temporal power was united in the pope. If Innocent's words could have meant to a contemporary merely that the pope was claiming jurisdiction when some "ambiguity" arose concerning a case which was "concurrently within the jurisdiction of both spiritual and temporal courts," either Laurentius or Vincentius or Johannes would have been delighted to point out the fact. None of them did so. Laurentius, the only one who referred specifically to the words of Deuteronomy in his glosses on *Per Venerabilem*, did maintain that the text was not necessarily a vindication of Alanus's extreme hierocratic doctrine of papal power, but he adopted a different line of argument to establish his point. . . . The distinction Laurentius made was not between secular cases and mixed cases but between appellate jurisdiction and ordinary jurisdiction, Alanus, on the other hand, maintained that the pope was "the ordinary judge . . . both as far as spiritual matters and temporal affairs."

The argument that ecclesiastical courts could exercise jurisdiction in mixed cases (the so-called *ratio connexitatis*) was, of course, not unfamiliar to canonists of the early thirteenth century. Indeed one may doubt whether Innocent would have thought it necessary to invoke Peter and Paul and an Old Testament prophet to establish such a relatively modest claim. We can demonstrate further that he conveyed a different meaning to contemporaries by considering some comments on the *ratio connexitatis* itself. From about 1215 onwards it became a common practice among the decretalists to present lengthy lists of all the cases in which papal jurisdiction could be exercised in the temporal sphere. Such lists invariably mentioned the *ratio connexitatis,* and they invariably mentioned the decretal, *Per Venerabilem.* But they did not cite *Per Venerabilem* in support of the claim to jurisdiction *ratione connexitatis;* it was always cited as the basis of a quite different claim. Thus Tancred wrote (citing Laurentius in the first part of his gloss):

This is one case in which the ecclesiastical judge can concern himself with matters of secular jurisdiction, namely when no superior is to be found. Another is when the secular judge neglects to render judgment or do justice. A third is when any matter is difficult and ambiguous and the judges differ, as below in the title *Qui filii sint legitimi, Per venerabilem.* La(urentius). Fourth, when it is a matter of land subject to the jurisdiction of the church. . . . Fifth, if it is according to custom. . . . Sixth, in all ecclesiastical crimes. . . . Seventh, when any case is referred to the church through denunciation by reason of crime, as above in the previous title, *Novit.* Eighth, when the secular judge is suspect and accused. . . . Ninth is the reason of connection, for an ecclesiastical judge can judge concerning dowry by reason of the fact that he has jurisdiction in matrimonial cases, as above in the title *De dote post divortium, De prudentia.*

This gloss was copied with little variation by Goffredus Tranensis and Bernardus Parmensis, and its substance repeated by Innocent IV and Hostiensis. Each of them cited the decretal *De Prudentia* on the law of dowry to illustrate the *ratio connexitatis,* while each cited *Per Venerabilem* in support of the much more vague and far-reaching claim to a jurisdiction in secular cases whenever the issues proved "ambiguous"

or "difficult" or when the judges were at odds with one another.

Finally, when the canonists did come to gloss in detail the words "Tria quippe distinguit iudicia" ["There are, to be sure, three distinct kinds of cases"] their interpretations regularly explained the third judgment as referring to cases which were *either* secular *or* spiritual, not both secular and spiritual at the same time. Innocent IV described the three judgments in this fashion:

Sanguinem [Blood]. A judgment is between blood and blood when the accuser says it is proved that the defendant has shed blood, that is, has committed any civil crime, let us say homicide, adultery, theft or anything of that sort. *Inter lepram et lepram* [Between leper and leper]. When the accuser says, "You are infected with the leprosy of heresy," that is, with any ecclesiastical crime, let us say simony, sacrilege, or anything similar, and the accused denies it. *Inter causam et causam* [Between case and case]. When the plaintiff says, "You owe me [a sum] from a loan or contract," or some similar civil action. Or, again, [when the plaintiff says] "You are bound to pay tithes to me" or "I have the right of patronage in this church," or some similar civil and ecclesiastical action, but the defendant denies it. For in all these matters, if anything shall be difficult or ambiguous recourse is to be had to the apostolic see.

There were thus really four types of cases involved — criminal actions which could be either ecclesiastical or secular, and civil actions which could likewise be divided into ecclesiastical cases or secular cases. The lack of symmetry in Innocent III's exposition in which both types of civil suit were lumped together under one heading arose simply from the structure of the text of Deuteronomy that he was expounding.

Hostiensis and Abbas Antiquus reproduced almost verbatim the comment of Innocent IV and a very similar explanation was given by Boatinus Mantuanus. I do not think that there can be any question here of a "hierocratic" distortion of Innocent III's original meaning. No other meaning had been suggested. The mid-thirteenth-century canonists were merely giving concrete examples to illustrate an interpretation that had been taken for granted by their predecessors. The principal reason why a modern reader might suppose that the third type of jurisdiction was intended to apply only to mixed cases lies in the fact that the immediate occasion of the decretal was a matter of legitimization, which did fall into this category. But, in the paragraph that we have been considering, Innocent III had turned aside from the issue of Count William's offspring to offer some general observations about the nature and extent of papal jurisdiction. It was not the habit of the canonists to relate such observations solely to the subject matter of the decretal in which they occurred; rather they sought to educe from them general rules of law, as in the comments of Tancred just cited. Innocent III himself was of course well aware of this decretalist technique. In general, it seems to me, the argument that Innocent's true meanings were misunderstood or distorted by the canonists of the next generation should be viewed with extreme caution. The pope was himself a trained canonist and a legislator of genius. He knew exactly what legal implications the canonists would find in the terms he chose to use, and we must surely suppose that he had a shrewd understanding of the effects they were likely to have on the long-range growth of canonical thought.

A new period in the study of Innocent's political ideas began with the publication in 1940 of Maccarrone's *Chiesa e stato,* the first work that seriously attempted to analyze his thought within its canonistic framework. Subsequently major contributions by Mochi Onory, Kempf, Stickler, and Tillmann have clarified our understanding of many doubtful points. It seems arguable, however, that all of these writers have been unduly influenced in their exegesis of *Per Venerabilem* by a natural inclination to defend Pope Innocent III against the charge of seeking worldly power as an end in itself. They are anxious, that is to say, to establish that the great pope was not actuated by motives of gross worldly ambition, but that all his interventions in the political sphere were inspired "by motives of a spiritual order" (a favorite phrase of Mochi Onory). Let us acknowledge at once that Innocent's intentions were probably of the best. It is, heaven knows, no mean task to try to build the City of God on earth. But it also remains true that, after his pontificate, many theologians and some popes did become committed to a doctrine of papal temporal power that was repugnant to the consciences (as well as the interests) of most mediaeval princes and prelates, that this papal claim produced a destructive tension in mediaeval Catholicism, and that Innocent III's decretals played a significant part in its development. The problem of whether he had good intentions is one issue, primarily psychological; the problem of what exactly he did claim in the secular sphere is another, primarily canonical. Both are important, but to endeavor to solve the second problem merely on the basis of a conviction about the first leads only to confusion.

This seems especially the fault of Mochi Onory. Above all he failed to see — and this is true of Maccarrone too — that there was a radical difference between a papal claim to exercise indirect power in temporal affairs and a claim to exercise direct power in certain exceptional circumstances which the pope himself undertook to define. It was quite consistent with the dualist theory to emphasize that an exercise of spiritual jurisdiction by the pope might sometimes, indirectly, produce effects in the temporal sphere. A sentence of excommunication launched against a king for some specifically ecclesiastical offense like sacrilege might, for example, have political repercussions. But it was surely not consistent with the dualist position for a pope to claim that he could exercise jurisdiction in secular cases whenever the case happened to be a "difficult and ambiguous" one (as was claimed in *Per Venerabilem*) or whenever the temporal judge was negligent or suspect or the office of emperor vacant (as Innocent suggested in the decretal *Licet*):

> If he gives up his power, if he neglects, is doubtful, or is a suspect judge . . .

as Hostiensis put it, summarizing Innocent III's doctrine.

It is hard to see how a pope could claim to judge secular cases even in such circumstances, or to enforce his sentences with coercive sanctions, unless he supposed that the nature of his office was such as to include jurisdiction over the purely temporal issues involved. Helene Tillmann is the only modern writer who has emphasized the important distinction between indirect power and direct power exercised *in certis causis*, but even she obscured its full implications by maintaining that the papal claim was rooted in the mediaeval doctrine of necessity. Innocent III certainly did know the Roman law tag, "Necessitas legem non habet [Necessity has no regard for law.]," and he could have used it as the basis of a claim to temporal jurisdiction in exceptional circumstances. But the fact is that he did not choose to do so. The legal doctrine of necessity, if applied to the transfer of cases between secular and ecclesiastical courts, might have had uncomfortable consequences. It could after all have worked both ways. No thirteenth-century pope would have conceded that the emperor could judge a spiritual case (on the ground that "necessitas legem non habet") whenever the ecclesiatical judges found the matter "difficult and ambiguous" or when the papacy happened to be vacant. Innocent III, therefore, preferred to base his claim on the quite different ground that he was the vicar of one who was a priest after the order of Melchisedech — and Melchisedech was of course both priest and king. On this theory the pope could judge secular cases when he considered it appropriate to do so simply because regal jurisdiction inhered in his office (and, correspondingly, the emperor could not judge spiritual cases because he possessed no spiritual jurisdiction).

Friedrich Kempf avoided this conclusion in his discussion of *Per Venerabilem* by stressing the voluntary nature of the jurisdiction involved. He did not argue that Innocent was claiming merely *iurisdictio voluntaria* in the most technical sense of that term (as opposed to *iurisdictio contentiosa* [jurisdiction involving a real legal problem], but he did maintain that, in *Per Venerabilem*, Innocent asserted the right to judge a secular case only when all the parties in the case voluntarily selected him as an arbitrator. There seems nothing in the decretal itself to support such a view. Its tone is quite different — "cum aliquid fuerit difficile vel ambiguum ad iudicium est sedis apostolicae recurrendum cuius sententiam qui superbiens contempserit observare mori praecipitur. . . . " Kempf also argued that *Per Venerabilem* must be interpreted in the light of Alexander III's decretal *Cum Sacrosancta*, and so understood in a dualist sense. In this earlier decretal Alexander replied to a series of questions from the archbishop of Rheims. The last one enquired whether an appeal from a secular judge to the pope was valid and the pope replied: "even if the (appeal) is valid according to ecclesiastical custom, we do not think it valid according to the strict meaning of the law." Kempf sees in this a definitive acknowledgment by the papacy of the autonomy of secular jurisdiction. Alexander did not, however, make any pronouncement at all in his decretal on the essentially theological issue of the inherent temporal power which might, or might not, be attributed to the papacy on the basis of such scriptural texts as Matthew xvi. 19. He indicated only that, as a matter of law, there was no adequate basis in the existing canons for a general right of appeal (though the custom of a local church sufficed to make the appeal valid). It was quite open to a future pope, who held on theological grounds that Christ had conferred on the papacy a supreme temporal jurisdiction, to enact such canons as he thought necessary to define the circumstances in which that jurisdiction would in fact be exercised. That is exactly what Innocent III did.

A. M. Stickler has insisted that the very occurrence in canonistic works of lists of "exceptional" cases in which secular jurisdiction would be exercised directly by the pope proves that, even in mid-thirteenth century, the canonists acknowledged in principle the autonomy of the secular power; and he suggested that the presence of such lists in the writings of extreme hierocrats like Tancred and Hostiensis reflects an unresolved tension in their thought. It is true that some dualist writers did hold that the fact of papal jurisdiction in secular cases being exercised only occasionally and in exceptional circumstances constituted an argument in favor of their own point of view. But their position was a very uneasy and illogical one, and it was natural enough that, after a generation's discussion of Innocent III's legislation, a major shift had occurred in canonistic thinking from the prevailing dualism of the late twelfth century to the dominant hierocratism of the mid-thirteenth. As we have argued, some of the "exceptional" cases were consistent with a dualist position, but some were not. On the other hand, the detailed definition of specific cases in which papal jurisdiction would be exercised directly in temporal affairs was entirely consistent with the most extreme hierocratic theories. Any court that claims a supreme appellate jurisdiction needs to define the circumstances in which it will in fact entertain appeals. It is quite possible to possess jurisdiction legitimately without exercising it in all cases; it is not possible to exercise jurisdiction legitimately in any case without possessing it. We may add that the listing of these exceptional cases occurs not only in the works of the canonists (whose technique of presenting scattered comments on a given topic in widely separated contexts could easily lead to inconsistencies), but also in the orderly exposition of the hierocratic theme by a systematic philosopher like Giles of Rome, who evidently saw no inconsistency in this

procedure. Giles maintained that all power, spiritual and temporal, was vested in the pope, that sometimes he wielded his temporal authority directly but more commonly permitted it to be exercised by secular rulers. He went on to mention seven specific cases (based on the canonical exceptions) where the pope actually exercised the universal temporal jurisdiction that pertained to his office, one of them being the "hard and doubtful" matter referred to in the decretal *Per Venerabilem*. Once again there is no question here of a hierocratic distortion of the pope's original meaning. Innocent himself had indeed spelled out precisely the same doctrine towards the end of *Per Venerabilem* itself: "Paul also, that he might expound the plenitude of power, wrote to the Corinthians saying, 'Do you not know that you shall judge angels? How much more the things of this world.' And so [the pope] is accustomed to exercise the office of secular power sometimes and in some things through himself, sometimes and in some things through others."

Innocent did not consider it appropriate or desirable to exercise his jurisdiction over spiritual affairs and over temporal affairs in precisely the same fashion, and he pointed this out in *Per Venerabilem*. In the ecclesiastical sphere he was *iudex ordinarius omnium*; in the temporal sphere he had no intention of burdening the papal curia with a mass of petty feudal litigation that, by legitimate custom, belonged to the courts of secular rulers. He did want to ensure that the temporal jurisdiction of the papacy could be invoked whenever a secular case had political implications involving the peace and good order of Christendom, and his various decretals provided a canonical basis for appeals in all such cases. Again, Innocent did take it for granted that, under the pope, secular rulers had a permanent and necessary role to play in the governance of Christian society, and that this role was a part of the divinely ordered scheme of things. He assumed that two hierarchies of administration were necessary for the government of the Christian world but, in his view, both hierarchies culminated in the pope. If this constitutes dualism, as some modern students of Innocent's thought seem to suppose, then all the mediaeval popes and all the most papalist of mediaeval theologians were dualists. It did not occur to Innocent III or his successors that it lay within their competence simply to abolish the offices of all secular rulers and themselves assume the exercise of all temporal power. But it also lay quite outside their competence, in the ecclesiastical sphere itself, to abolish the office of bishop and rule all the affairs of the church through papal delegates. Either innovation would have grievously perturbed "the general state of the church," which was not permitted to a pope or any human legislator.

The recent work on Pope Innocent III has been much concerned with relating his ideas to their mediaeval background. This is all to the good. It needs to be emphasized that the theory of papal power he propounded bore little resemblance to modern positivist theories of sovereignty and still less to modern totalitarian theories of despotism. We shall, however, eventually come to a full understanding of Innocent's position, not by minimizing his plainly stated claim to temporal power, but by relating that claim to the complex of doctrines concerning natural law, counsel and consent, *status ecclesiae,* and customary rights that mediaeval popes, as well as their critics, took for granted.

The Man

HELENE TILLMANN

Helene Tillmann (1896—   ) received her doctorate at Bonn and is currently teaching at the Kaiserin-Augusta-Schule. Her deep sympathy with Innocent III permeates all of her published work. In the following passage, she examines the character and personality of the pope, finding him a warm and witty human being. Her estimate of Innocent's personality, so sharply in conflict with that of Johannes Haller, furnishes us with ample opportunity and material for considering the question how far Innocent III's policies and ideals flowed directly from his personality and to what extent they were irreconcilable with it. This selection also rounds out our portrait of the many-faceted career of Innocent by focusing attention on the man himself.

I N August, 1202, Innocent stopped for a while in Subiaco. We have a happy find by Karl Hampe to thank for a description of this sojourn. It is a letter which a higher official of the curia, but not a cardinal, wrote from Subiaco to an absent colleague. The report makes a witty but genuinely perceptive complaint about the hardships there, to which the curia was exposed under the hot sun of Subiaco. Above the sea, enclosed by rugged, gloomy mountains, lay the place where the tents for the pope, the officials of the curia, and the baggage were pitched. On the south side, the cook had set up his smoky tent. The wrangling of the kitchen help over tallow and grease continually resounded. On the East, the apothecary held his flasks of urine up to the heavens in the morning, while all day long he disturbed his surroundings by the unpleasantly monotonous pounding of his mortar. On the North, the crowd of buyers and sellers streamed to market in the early morning. Their wrangling and crying put an end to sleep. The members of the curia were tired, and they remained tired all day. Often the pope, whose shabby tent was pitched on the west side, saw his fellow-worker sleeping over his work. In spite of the cool breeze from the sea, the heat was hard to bear. From sunrise on, the gnats, whose hum itself was a torture, harassed them; from early morning the song of the cicadas disturbed their sleep. Night brought the chirping of the crickets to the despair of sensitive nerves. No less did the groans and wailing of those lying all round oppress them. On the other hand, the view of the sea was magnificent. The chaplains frequently refreshed themselves in its cool water so that they seemed to live like fish. The letter-writer described the sea as, for the most part, a tantalizing torture; he was afraid of the neck-breaking descent and the exhausting re-ascent, which blotted out of his memory the pleasures that the sea held out.

Innocent experienced hardships in the provisional camp under the hot sun of Subiaco that were hardly less than those of the letter-writer. We know that he had to forego mass and preaching in Monte Cassino on account of the increasing sultriness brought to the point of intolerability by the crowd of people. The summer

From Helene Tillmann, *Papst Innocenz III* (Bonn: Ludwig Röhrscheid Gmbh., 1954), pp. 233–42; 255–57. By permission of the publisher. Translated by the editor.

months were always extremely critical for his generally poor health. For that reason, he spent them outside of Rome when no special demands made his presence in the city necessary. In Subiaco, Innocent was able to escape many hardships behind the protective walls of the monastery. But he wanted to share them openly with his retinue and perhaps he did not wish to be a burden to the monastery. In his modest simplicity, defying the hardships of the place and of the season, he was content with a shabby tent or a simple hut; he did not desire any special regard from his companions, but took the buzzing, crying, and groaning with apparent patience. The members of the curia could flee to him if the torture of the heat became unbearable. In the words of the letter-writer, they forced him, like themselves, to rest from work and, sitting intimately at his feet in stimulating conversation, they forgot the summer torture.

Thus, Innocent does not stand before us as a man unapproachable in his sense of the dignity of his office and in his consciousness of the oppressive burden of his responsibilities. The letter-writer, with a smile of intimacy yet in the respectful language of the curia, speaks also of Innocent as the third Solomon, our most reverend father, the successor of the prince of the apostles and the representative of Jesus Christ, the spring of all living waters, to whom have been allotted the treasures of all wisdom and eloquence. He also discovers important trifles about the pope; the third Solomon likes to live on islands in the sea and, therefore, he is not afraid of the dangerous descent and the exhausting ascent as the writer is. He dips his "holy hands" into the water and uses it as a refreshing gargle. When the writer tells us that he consulted the physician for a sick friend, he does not neglect to add that the third Solomon also esteems the doctor. Visitors to the curia, like the letter-writer, confirm the fact of Innocent's affable, humanly simple nature and his amiability. A monk from the monastery of St. Andrew, near

Boulogne, relates with still happy memory the story of his audience with the pope. He approached Innocent when he was just awaking from his afternoon nap and was still free of business. Just as the monk was kneeling down, Innocent called him, greeted him with a kiss, and, after finishing his business, told about his visit to the monastery of St. Andrew, whose hospitality he had enjoyed when he had made a pilgrimage to the tomb of St. Thomas of Canterbury while he was a student in Paris. During the Christmas season, Innocent twice sent game to the monk Thomas Marleberg of Evesham. It was not the first time that the pope did small favors for strangers who spent some time at the curia. His pleasant nature was revealed by his attendance at the tournament held in his honor by the men of Ceccano while he was on a trip to the southern borders of the papal state and by the way he enjoyed the sport of the young men in Viterbo, as it is reported. In the vivid description of Gerald of Wales, the famous writer who visited the curia, Innocent appears in the same kind and humanly simple way. Once, on an outing to Fonte Vergine, Innocent talked with him for a long time both seriously and in a humorous vein. He laughed heartily about the rough way in which Gerald indicted for slander a monk who thought Gerald had stolen his horse. Gerald even wants us to believe that Innocent joined him and the cardinals in making fun of the poor Latin and lack of theological education of Hubert Walter, the Archbishop of Canterbury, who opposed him in a lawsuit. Undoubtedly, the gentleman from Wales is lying here, as he was in his dispute with the archbishop; those remarks he later retracted as mostly gossip. Innocent could not forget the special dignity and consideration due an outstanding member of the episcopate. Social frivolity certainly did not mean that one could let oneself go completely. He possessed a definite sense of what was fitting and proper. When, after the death of Pope Celestine III, some of the cardinals fled the Lateran to find greater safety in the Septizonium for the preparations for the new election, he was one of the cardinals who remained until the end in the Lateran in order to participate in the funeral of the pope. Feelings of personal intimacy were not important in influencing him to do this, for he was never, by any means, close to the deceased. We learn that now and then Innocent had the cross carried before him as he took a walk; he did not, therefore, try to escape the obligations to which he was bound as holder of his high office, even while he was relaxing. Gerald might be right in his assumption that it was hard for Innocent to hide his smile at Gerald's witty but malicious pranks. Innocent liked to have the company of this intelligent fellow, but did not take him too seriously because of his boundless vanity and his imperturbable cockiness, as well as the almost childish manner in which he displayed both. Gerald himself noticed once how Innocent, shaking his head at Gerald's speech, cast a smile at Cardinal Hugolino, who was seated at his side.

Gerald is not the only one who recorded the happy trait of wit and humor in the character of the pope. A visitor to the curia observed how Innocent turned in the middle of official business to tell a joke in Italian. Once when a proctor complained that his opponents had stolen his lawyers, Innocent answered with a smile that no one ever lacked legal advisers at the Roman curia. O what a happy event! he supposedly exclaimed when he heard the news that Archbishop John of Trier, whose vacillation did not permit him to attend the court of the Hohenstaufen or to stay away, had fallen from his horse. Even if it is only an anecdote, it confirms, as does another told by Salimbene, the view of the pope's humor held by contemporaries and by posterity. The Franciscan reports the amusing conversation of the pope with a witty fellow, whom Innocent answered in the same poor Latin in which he had been addressed, and he adds that the pope was a man who sometimes permitted himself joy among his sorrows. Now and then, Innocent's sense of humor was expressed in the more biting form of irony. He wanted to give the Bishop of Fiesole a chance to find out if he could, as he boasted, bribe the pope to forgive him. "Look here, Adam was created like one of us . . ." he stated ironically when the Bishop of Penne forgot, on his promotion, that he was bound to follow a simple life especially since he was a Cistercian. At the same time he reminded him of the words of Genesis, "I am sorry for having created man." Innocent did not consider it irony, but a kind of joke, when in his chambers he once addressed Gerald of Wales — who was working at the curia for recognition of his election to the bishopric of St. David's and also for metropolitan status for the diocese — as elect of St. David's and at another time as archbishop.

The Welsh author, to whom we owe so many exciting details of Innocent's private life, also furnishes particulars about the pope's interests. Once when poems were recited in honor of the pope and in his presence, Gerald received the most applause for his poem. It is not a false generalization to assume that the recitation of poetry or readings from scripture were a part of the social program at the papal court. Innocent was well acquainted with classical literature and had some notion of the grandeur of Greek culture. For him, Athens was the city from which much learning streamed out to almost every corner of the world, the city with a brilliant name and of complete beauty, the city which first taught the art of philosophy and which brought forth poets, the mother of all the arts, the city of learning. He had at least some knowledge of Greek.

It is significant that Gerald, who was extraordinarily well read and looked down arrogantly on others because of his own educational background and learning, acknowledged the breadth of the pope's reading and praised him as a lover of literature, and not merely of theology. We can also believe the contemporary biographer of the pope when he stresses the pope's education in secular matters. Gerald often had occasion to talk with Innocent. On one visit to the curia, he presented him with six of his writings. As the author proudly relates, Innocent had them lying beside his bed for nearly a month. The pope pointed out the fine points of style and content to the cardinals who visited him and finally lent them out to them one by one. He did not want to give up one work, the *Gemma Ecclesiastica,* however. Certainly Gerald exaggerated — because of his vanity as an author — but in fact the exciting works, namely the topography and conquest of Ireland along with the *Gemma,* must have interested the brilliant mind of the pope. It is a proof of the pontiff's noble impartiality that he enjoyed a book such as the *Gemma Ecclesiastica* or allowed himself to receive it with a smile. A lesser mind would have taken offense at the writing. The author expressed doubts about coercing the clergy to be celibate, repeated, in the midst of attacks on the worldly possessions of the church, the legend that the devil had exclaimed triumphantly on the day of the Donation of Constantine: "I have injected a poison into the church," and hinted at the immoderate financial burden of prelates because of their expenses at the curia and for the cardinals, their relatives, and legates.

The close connections of the pope with the Universities of Paris and Bologna testify to his lively interest in learning. His historical knowledge and his high critical ability appear to us as remarkable for his time. He had probably acquired this knowledge in part while studying in the papal archives. He was able to train his critical faculties and his then rare sense of historical development and use them for the comparison of source materials, an opportunity which the curia offered in a unique manner.

Innocent III had as keen an appreciation of the plastic arts as he did of literature and poetry. He had added a peristyle to the church of SS. Sergius and Bacchus,

reconstructed by him during his years as a cardinal. He also undertook extensive alterations in the Lateran and Vatican palaces. The hospital of the Holy Spirit was rebuilt by him and, in the name of his brother, Richard of Segni, the huge tower later called the *Torre dei Conti* was erected. The hospital and the tower were praised by later generations as masterpieces. When an earthquake destroyed the tower in the time of Petrarch, the poet lamented the collapse of this unique building. Innocent had the mosaics in the ceiling of the apse of St. Peter's renovated and had his portrait put in — this reminds us of the popes of the Renaissance. He donated valuable products of the goldsmith's art, illustrated books, and embroidery to churches within and outside of Rome, or he contributed to their restoration and structural embellishment. In the judgment of experts, he united Roman majesty and aesthetic sensitivity to the best effect in the execution of his papal bulls. The "E" in the *Ego* of the papal signature and the small cross done by the pope himself are outstanding because of their beautiful clear lines. The same fine perception of forms and sureness and firmness of line already distinguished the signature of the cardinal-deacon of SS. Sergius and Bacchus.

This picture of the rich and varied personality of Innocent III is complete with the discovery that he was an able singer and wrote songs well and that his ear was sensitive to dissonant voices and harsh sounds. . . .

History has denied Innocent III its highest distinction, the title of great. Decisions of this kind are irrevocable. Would we appeal if it were possible? Must not the fact that Innocent III led the spiritual and temporal power of the mediaeval papacy to its highest point and that he, unlike his successor, had put substance in his claims ensure him of the claim to commanding greatness?

He performed in a commanding manner when he strengthened the papacy in the new papal states and in its feudal vassal-state of Sicily in the face of historical events. That his successors in great part weakly surrendered this strength, which like all strength was a relative thing, did not diminish the accomplishment of Innocent III. His efforts for church freedom and his work of reform, as well as the protection and promotion he gave the pathbreaking Catholic poverty movement, are witnesses for his spiritual greatness. If the Catholic Church had nothing else to thank Innocent for than this protection and the issuance of a doctrine which still binds the church today, *i.e.*, to receive the sacrament of the Eucharist at least once a year, the great significance of his pontificate for the development of Christian life in the church would be assured. Innocent's rule has become distinguished for the further spread of canon law. It marked a turning-point in the history of Germany, England, Italy, and France. The preparation of two crusades was an important, if in the final analysis, fruitless, accomplishment. And the man on whose shoulders the burden of work, worry, and the accountability lay, who was surrounded by the events and decisions of his pontificate, was a man in poor health, who more than once in the eighteen years of his pontificate had been extremely ill. The establishment and preservation of papal rule in Rome and the states of the church, the work of strengthening the Patrimony, and the papal regency in Sicily put an endlessly exhausting and grinding round with a thousand problems and a thousand often malicious impediments in the way. The ordinary problems of administration and jurisdiction would have been almost enough of a strain, given the conscientious attention with which Innocent discharged them. In less important matters, too, no real decision could be made by the chancery without his knowledge. He drew up his own letters, insofar as they were not purely formal, either completely or for the most part.

The faculty for sharply critical thought and for strong and determined action as well as a high degree of feeling for his limitations attest to Innocent's statesmanlike and human talents. He set clear goals for himself and held them fixedly before his eyes, but he was to a great degree flexible in the selection of ways and the preparation of means. Fundamentally conservative, he did not slam the door on fruitful new things, and he himself also pioneered new paths. He united the knowledge of duty, need, and the idealistic goal to a calm sense of the true, the possible, and the attainable.

Posterity, which refused Innocent the title of great, might take it into account that, he, with all the foresight with which he worked for the future, was still not always able to rise above his time and its immediate circumstances. The not unmerited failures of his policy in the Fourth Crusade and on the question of the union of the churches or the ambiguity of his position with respect to the crusade against heresy could possibly be an objection to his acceptance as a commanding historical and personal great.

Ideas of such kind, however, can hardly explain why Innocent does not live on in history as a great. The personality of a pope should not be evaluated only by the measure of his greatness as a statesman; it must also and before all be measured according to the obligations of his office and his worthiness as a vicar of Christ. In part, Innocent was suited to these. With a holy fervor, he had worked for the reform of the clergy and the Church; the purification of the church was his ardent desire and the object of fixed concern of his pontificate. He had a deep sense of his obligations as guardian of the faith and the moral law. His priestly life was irreproachable; his piety was genuine and deep. But he did not always act from the highest religious interpretation of his office; still, he did not often sacrifice the values of law and morality, for which he had often acted with a high moral sense, to his political goals.

With a fine sense of value, perhaps, has history withheld the title of great from Innocent, who could not resolve the ambiguity between his role as vicar of Christ and statesman and politician, in spite of his commanding significance in world history. At the same time it singled out Leo I and Gregory I, popes, who are also numbered among the saints of the Catholic Church.

SUGGESTIONS FOR ADDITIONAL READING

The student who desires to pursue this subject further will almost immediately encounter the language barrier. The writings of Innocent himself remain for the most part untranslated from the original Latin. They have been collected by J. P. Migne in the closing volumes of his *Patrologia Latina* (Paris, 1844–1864). A critical edition of his *De Miseria Humane Conditionis* (Lucani, 1955) has been edited by Michele Maccarrone for the series *Thesaurus Mundi*. An important critical study of Innocent's letters is: Friedrich Kempf, *Die Register Innocenz III* (Rome, 1945). However, *Selected Letters of Pope Innocent III concerning England (1198–1216)* (Edinburgh, 1953) have been edited and translated into English by C. R. Cheney and W. H. Semple. These letters will permit students without facility in Latin an opportunity to study some of Innocent's actions and policies at first hand.

Fortunately, too, there are many fine works in English dealing with the mediaeval church and various aspects of its development. One of the best brief surveys is contained in M. Baldwin's *The Medieval Church* (Ithaca, N.Y., 1953). Gustav Schnurer's *L'Église et la Civilisation* published in two volumes (Paris, 1933–35) has been translated into English under the title *The Church and Culture in the Middle Ages* (Paterson, N.J., 1956–). Walter Ullmann's study of the *Growth of Papal Government in the Middle Ages* (London, 1955) is probably the best introduction to ecclesiastical administration in any language. His work might be supplemented by R. L. Poole's *Lectures on the History of the Papal Chancery down to the Time of Innocent III* (Cambridge, England, 1915) and W. E. Lunt's *Financial Relations of the Papacy with England to 1327* (Cambridge, Mass., 1939) and his *Papal Revenues in the Middle Ages* (2 vols. New York, 1934). *Western Canon Law* (Berkeley, 1953) by R. C. Mortimer is one of the few studies of this important aspect of the church available in English. For the post-Innocentian development of the church, A. Flick's *Decline of the Medieval Church* is indispensable.

There are so many important studies of the church in other languages that it is impossible to do anything more than to select arbitrarily a few of the more important ones. Augustin Fliche and V. Martin edited and contributed to the *Histoire de l'Église depuis les Origines à nos Jours* (Paris, 1934–). However, the quality of scholarship in this series is somewhat irregular. Fliche himself published a very fine manual, *La Chrétienté Médiévale* (Paris, 1929). His major work, however, remains the *Réforme grégorienne* (3 vols. Louvain, 1927–37), a truly significant background work to any study of Innocent III. The papacy is the central focus of Ferdinand Gregorovious, *Geschichte der Stadt Rom im Mittelalter* (8 vols. Stuttgart, 1859–72), which remains, from a literary point of view, one of the great monuments of German historiography. C. J. Hefele's *Conciliengeschichte* (7 vols. Freiburg, 1855–74) is much more than a history of the councils; it is a major study of the doctrinal development of the church. There is a French translation by Leclerq and a partial English translation by W. R. Clark (Edinburgh, 1871–96). Johannes Haller's *Das Papsttum* (5 vols., 2nd ed., Esslingen, 1962) provides a sharply contrasting viewpoint on most issues to that of Hefele or of Fliche. For a listing of more specialized works in English or other languages, the student should consult L. J. Paetow's *Guide to the Study of Medieval History* (New York, 1959). Since Paetow does not list books printed after 1930, the student ought also to consult *Speculum: A Journal of*

Mediaeval Studies for reviews of more recent works. For more serious work, there are numerous bibliographies, many of which are listed in Paetow and *Speculum*.

The best brief study of Innocent III in English is still S. R. Packard's *Europe and the Church under Innocent III* (New York, 1927), in spite of the fact that it is now long out of date and many of its generalizations are open to question. The biography of Innocent by Leonard Elliott-Binns (London, 1931) suffers from the same difficulty. Joseph Clayton's *Innocent III and his Times* (Milwaukee, 1941) is rather uncritical; it belongs to the genre of apologetics rather than scholarly history. Charles Smith's *Innocent III, Church Defender* (Baton Rouge, 1951) is valuable insofar as it focuses attention on an aspect of Innocent's career that has received scant notice in earlier English works. Innocent has not received the serious attention of English-speaking scholars writing for learned journals.

However, the paucity of materials in English is compensated for by the numerous studies in other languages. Most of the selections in this book have been taken from authors whose work has been previously untranslated. The student would be well advised to continue his reading on Innocent by consulting the complete works from which the selections have been taken. Achille Luchaire's *Innocent III* (6 vols. Paris, 1905–08) is still an indispensable beginning for a fuller understanding of this pope. There are also many studies dealing with limited aspects of Innocent's reign or with special problems of the period. W. Norden's *Das Papsttum und Byzanz* (Berlin, 1903), while not limited to the period of Innocent III, provides much valuable information on his relations with the East. Friedrich Baethgen has discussed Innocent's influence over the young Hohenstaufen, Frederick II, and evaluated his

performance of this duty in *Die Regentschaft Papst Innocenz III im Königreich Sizilien* (Heidelberg, 1914). Else Gütschow explored his relations with John Lackland in *Innocenz III und England* (Munich, 1904). Two studies of Innocent's relations with Germany are still interesting: E. Engelmann, *Philipp von Schwaben und Papst Innocenz III während des deutschen Thronstreites* (Berlin, 1896) and R. Schwemer, *Innocenz III und die deutsche Kirche während des Thronstreites von 1198–1208* (Strasburg, 1882).

There is a wide and interesting literature concerned with Innocent's conception of the relations between church and state. The classic work in English is A. J. and R. W. Carlyle, *Mediaeval Political Theory in the West* (5 vols. Edinburgh, 1903–28). Michele Maccarrone's *Chiesa e stato nella dottrina di Innocenzo III* (Rome, 1940) presents a well-developed argument against the idea that Innocent claimed temporal power beyond the papal states. Also, consult F. Kempf, *Papsttum und Kaisertum bei Innocenz III* (Rome, 1954). Many scholars have been especially interested in the origins of the papal ideas about the state. S. Mochi Onory has investigated these in his *Fonti canonistiche dell'idea moderna dello stato* (Milan, 1951). W. Ullmann's *Medieval Papalism: The Political Theories of the Medieval Canonists* (London, 1949) is an important study in English from a somewhat different point of view.

The number of works cited here is relatively few, and the topics for which titles are given do not begin to cover all aspects of Innocent's manifold interests and accomplishments. However, the footnotes and bibliographies to these works will provide the student with many more books and articles which will enable him to pursue his interest further.